KEEP THE FLAME ALIVE

How to Help Your Marriage
Survive and Thrive

By Karen Gadke, Ph.D

Willowcreek MedCom
an imprint of
Willowcreek Enterprises
Capron, Illinois

Published by:

Willowcreek MedCom, an imprint of
Willowcreek Enterprises
Capron, Illinois

Cover Design: Cindy Bartosiak

Copy Editor: Barb Iehl

Cover Photo: Donald R. Vaughan, Jr.

ISBN No. 0-9661624-0-4

To order KEEP THE FLAME ALIVE, send
$10.95 plus $2.- for S&H to:
Willowcreek MedCom, P.O. Box 133,
Capron, Il. 61012. Illinois residents add
$0.68 sales tax. Discounts for orders of
10 books or more are available.

I dedicate this book to:

My husband Richard, for his patience, his acceptance of all my faults and idiosyncrasies, and for showing me, more in deeds than words, what love means.

My mother Klara, for her dedication and love, and for teaching me integrity, self-discipline, commitment and gratitude.

My furry four-legged friends, my sled dog team, for their unwavering loyalty and love, and for brightening up my life every day.

All those who are struggling to keep the flame alive in their marriage.

Last but not least, my Creator and His Holy Spirit, for seeing me through this work and all the other challenges of life.

Acknowledgments

I thank all those who have assisted me in writing this book:

Copy Editor Barb Iehl

Computer Consultant Jim Rathbun

Photographer Donald R. Vaughan, Jr.

Proofreader Linda A. Saue

My very special friends Sue Britton and John Rinaldo, and my former University mentor Kenneth Brownson, Ph.D., Ed.D, for reviewing my manuscript.

Pastor Terry Cowan for permission to take the cover photo at Flora Church, Kirkland, Il, and Jerimiah Nottingham and Christa Godfrey for permission to photograph their hands.

All others who have helped me in some way, and have kept me going with their encouragement. This includes those who have permitted me to put their personal stories into words so that others, including myself, can learn from their experience.

I also thank the authors and publishers who kindly gave me permission to quote some of their words and describe some of their concepts. They are listed under References/Recommended Reading and again in the Special Acknowledgments section at the end of this book.

Special Notes:

These pages describe certain traits shared by the majority of people. We all know that there are exceptions to every rule. If anyone feels labeled, I apologize.

This book does not describe how to cope with special problems, such as seemingly insurmountable ideological differences. They are beyond the scope of this book.

Stories told in this book are true. To protect privacy, the names and a few minor details have been changed.

TABLE OF CONTENTS

INTRODUCTION

Philosopher Bertrand Russell wrote,

"Those who have not known the deep intimacy and the intense companionship of happy mutual love have missed the best thing that life has to give."

Unfortunately, in their quest for fulfillment and self-gratification, many seem to have forgotten what caring, sharing love is.

The fifty percent divorce rate in the United States reflects this trend. And, if the upward spiral of the divorce rate continues, the family as we know it may be extinct in a few more decades.

This book was written to help change this trend, to stem the progression of this national, or rather, worldwide tragedy. I hope it will help couples to grow together rather than apart, to accept each other as they did when they first fell in love, sharing all the good things life has to offer. I hope and pray that those who read my words will renew their marriage vows, and that their happiness will spill over to their family, their friends, the community, the country, the whole world.

The research I did in preparation for the writing of these chapters has been a great learning experience for me. All of the books I have read on this subject, the many people I have talked to, and all those who have encouraged and helped me to put these pages together have been a great inspiration.

Writing this book has been a true journey of discovery. I have learned much about myself and my own marriage, and how to make it better every day.

I am eager to share with my readers what I have learned. I want so very much to help others learn and grow in their relationships, to experience the joys of love, the joys of living. So if, in my eagerness to accomplish this, I sound like I am lecturing, I apologize.

The book deals with ways to cope with problems or, better yet, their prevention. It explores many ways to *keep the fire burning*, to maintain zest and romance in your marriage. It stresses the importance of honesty, of sharing and relating, of physical affection and ego strokes.

If you say, "We have no problem," don't be so sure. In medicine, prevention is always less costly than the cure. And the same goes for relationships. It is wise to be careful, so as not to inflict wounds on your partner. Because, scar tissue tends to *act up* from time to time, and emotional scars can last a lifetime.

You might say, "I have already read many books on this subject." You will be surprised how much new insight you will gain from these pages. Besides, a little review may be just what you need to polish a few *rusty spots* you weren't aware of.

Even the best marriage can use some improvement. And those going through heartbreaking times need all the help they can get to work through their crises and dilemmas. No book holds the solution to every problem, but if you follow even a few of the suggestions made in these chapters, your relationship will be enhanced.

For those who want their lives together to be as happy as possible, this book is for you. If my words will help only one couple regain the joy they had in the beginning of their marriage, and if it will prevent only one broken heart and the destruction of one family, it will have been worth the effort.

In my work in both the medical and mental health fields I have seen many lives destroyed because people didn't know how to work out small differences. In many cases lack of proper communication skills was the culprit. Or, something that started as "just a little harmless flirting with a friend or colleague," developed into a tragedy for all those involved.

Adultery is rarely planned. Usually people fall into it because of opportunity, or sometimes because of loneliness. Someone who may otherwise not have been appealing suddenly *fills the gap*.

Awareness of your own vulnerability and remembering the little word "NO" when the opportunity presents itself could mean the difference between preserving your marriage or finding yourself in divorce court. It is far better to start working on your problems instead of running away from them.

There are no perfect marriages, and not many near-perfect ones. But those numbers can change if people will only work a little harder. If they will follow some of the suggestions in these chapters or other good books on this subject. Among the most important of these suggestions are, to love and forgive - yourself and your partner - and to forget about *an eye for an eye* if your partner has hurt you.

I have a vision for the future - one of renewed faith in the sacred institution of marriage, of children growing up securely enveloped by the love of a complete family: A mom and a dad who love, respect and honor each other. And I ask all of those who read my words to help me achieve this goal, so we can all live in a better world. Because, if we are ever to achieve peace in this world, peace in the family must come first.

My husband, Richard, and I believe we have a good marriage. But it has not always been without trouble. Staying happily married has involved hard work. After 21 years of marriage, I would not be truthful if I would say that there has never been any boredom or pain. But we decided to make needed adjustments, and to work at keeping romance alive, every day. We decided to work harder at focusing on each other's needs instead of just our own.

We decided to renew the choice we made when we said "I Do". We now choose to see the good in each other, even if we get angry and see the opposite at times. The traits that attracted us to each other when we first met are still there. We just have to look a little harder sometimes.

I am saddened to see so many of our friends and acquaintances break up, usually over matters that could have been resolved if the partners had practiced some *give and take*.

This book is written with one thought in mind, to help save marriages. I believe that most marriages could be saved if the partners would be willing to stay committed to their marriage vows. If they would not give in to the trend of the times, namely, to take the easy way out rather than work out their problems. IF THEY WOULD BE FAITHFUL TO EACH OTHER!

If you would renew your commitment to each other often, instead of heading for divorce court at the slightest sign of trouble, your children would be happier too. You may not realize this. Children, including young ones, perceive when things are not good between their parents. Even if the parents keep up a happy front, subtle body language tells all. And it troubles the children. They are the innocent victims of divorce.

Yes, getting married is the easy part, but it is much harder to stay married, and to remain happily married is the most difficult and also the most rewarding pursuit I know of. Are you ready to cash in on the rewards, *'til death do you part'*?

CHAPTER I

THE FRIENDLY ENEMIES

Although people never quite want to admit this, the male and female of the species of *homo sapiens* seem to be natural enemies. This love-hate relationship between men and women is as old as humanity itself. Recorded throughout history in literature, poetry and song, men and women claim they just can not get along without each other. Yet they often want to get away from each other, especially once they are bound together by marriage. Or so it seems.

It does not have to be that way. We need to understand the fundamental differences between male and female. After we gain an understanding of these basic differences and why they exist, we can more easily work out the problems arising from them. We can put a little tolerance to work and learn to respect some of our differences. We can learn the art of compromise.

How males and females handle their differences can mean the success or failure of a relationship. Since communication skills are of utmost importance here, the next chapter will be devoted to this art.

Vive La Difference

That's what they say. It is believed that this is what puts zip into relationships. Opposites attract. And it is this attraction that brings couples together at first.

So why is it that, after people live together for a while and get to know each

other better, some of the differences that
first attracted seem to get in the way? It
appears that couples just don't know how to
handle these differences once they have to
cope with them on a daily basis.

Why Do We Try to Change Each Other?

It is human nature to want others to
like the things we like, and to share our
beliefs and opinions. It is also human nature to be selfish. So, if differences in
opinion get in the way, people often resort
to fighting, or worse, they give up on the
marriage.
Is there another approach? You bet
there is. This approach combines two vital
factors: Understanding our fundamental differences, and communication.
Let's investigate some of these differences between males and females. Actually, they go back to the womb, to infancy,
and to the way our earliest and most powerful role models, namely our parents, influ-
enced us.

Right Brain - Left Brain

Based on studies conducted using heat-
sensitive color monitors, scientists now believe that, between the eighteenth and twen-
ty-sixth weeks of gestation, something happens to the brain of the developing male
fetus -- something that forever separates
the sexes.
What is this mysterious thing that
happens to the unborn male child?
It has to do with the two hemispheres
of the brain, the right side and the left
side, which are connected by a separating
part called the corpus callosum. Scientists
now believe that, under the influence of

sex-related hormones, some of the fibers in the corpus callosum of the male fetus which connect the two hemispheres are destroyed. Thus, boys are typically more left-brain oriented.

Little girls, on the other hand, are more **global** (two-sided) in their thinking. In other words, messages between the left and right brain travel faster and are less inhibited in girls, because the connections in the corpus callosum all remain intact.

Does this imply that boys are brain-damaged?

Not at all. It is simply meant to be that way so that males can specialize in predominantly left-brain thinking (more logical, factual, analytical), while females can be more specialized in right-brain thinking (artistic, intuitive, language/communication-oriented). This is why the female is more aware of relational needs, and finds it easier to talk about them.

So, males and females complement each other. Nature put this differentiation there for a reason. Every household functions best when there is one of each. We all need each other. So why not try to understand, instead of trying to change each other.

What Happens After Birth?

During infancy boys and girls are cuddled in the same manner. But as the little boy grows, differences in how we treat children begin to surface - at least in most families. For example, boys are told not to cry, while girls may cry all they want. And this is socially acceptable for the female, even into old age. But boys are told that they must not show weakness or softness, and they must certainly never cry.

Fortunately, this trend is changing, as men are beginning to exhibit more traits of humanness and vulnerability. But they have a long way to go.

Traditionally, the male child is taught early on that he is stronger and more courageous, and that he must protect the female. Even if the parents do not *hammer in* this concept, it is so well portrayed in films and books that the growing boy could not possibly escape it. Since the male is not allowed to show weakness or fear, he learns to *protect* his inner sanctum, never showing how he really feels, never showing vulnerability.

A man may hurt, but finds it too difficult to talk about it. This builds unnecessary stresses in his system. Thus he may act out in other, often hostile ways, simply because he needs to *blow off steam*.

Males Provide Protection, Females Receive It

We females are taught to let our men protect us. We can be vulnerable, and talk about our feelings and troubles without fear of being judged. Unless we work at changing them, the basic traits shaped in us during childhood remain with us through life.

There are times when people apply these basic traits to get what they want. The male may apply his power, or try to. The female, having been taught that she is weaker (and, when it comes to physical strength, she is) sometimes resorts to using *manipulation* if she wants something of the male.

These characteristics, whenever they are put to work, breed resistance and often resentment. He resents because he feels manipulated, she resents that she is usually in the *begging position*, and still doesn't always get what she wants. Quite often one partner or the other develops what is called passive resistance (*I'll do it, but not until I'm ready, certainly not at this moment, and most certainly not because you snap your finger*).

Feelings Of Resentment

The feelings of resentment resulting from this power struggle between male and female, if not dealt with, are buried in the unconscious mind and tend to cause trouble in the future.

If couples would try a little harder to understand each other, so much trouble could be avoided. If they would take into consideration the basic differences between males and females, and communicate their feelings openly, many problems could be solved before they become insurmountable.

Affection and Closeness

There are also differences in regard to affection and closeness. Generally, wives crave affection and can never get enough of it, while husbands are generally more interested in sex. Of course, there are exceptions to this rule, and some wives may be more aggressive sexually than their husbands. Generally, marital intimacy is so much easier for the female than the male. She craves it, while he may shy away from it.

Women Crave Affection, Men Need Space

Having received generally more cuddling during childhood, women continue to need the affection they are used to receiving. A man, on the other hand, may feel smothered when his partner gives and asks for more affection than he desires.

Many men can only handle so much closeness, and if this threshold is exceeded, they will pull away. A man in this state of mind may become silent, withdrawn, leave the house, work late, or whatever else he can think of to make some space for himself. If a man only knew how to explain this, so much trouble could be avoided. However, trying to keep up the image of being strong, being in command, usually prevents him from coming out with the truth.

A man's desire for space often makes a woman feel rejected or abandoned. Her need for intimacy is being ignored. Having always been protected and coddled -- at least in most families -- she finds it unacceptable to be ignored. Under stress, she may come to him asking for connection and comfort. Just a hug or two will often do it. If he doesn't get the message, feelings of loneliness, sadness or anxiety may set in.

A woman who feels she is being ignored by her husband may begin whining and nagging, making statements such as, "You don't love me." She may pick other topics to complain about, as did my friend Eileen.

Eileen related to me that whenever her husband Matthew *ignored* her several times in short succession, the inevitable *straw that broke the camel's back* would surface. At times like that Eileen would raise her voice and scream at him, "You are leaving clutter all over the house and you expect me to be the maid and clean up all your messes ..."

Accusations of this type, even if they seem justified, can start a repetitious downtrend in the relationship -- a vicious cycle of begging for affection, not receiving it, blaming and resenting and more com-

plaining by her, resulting in more withdrawal by him.

Seeing the Worst in Each-Other

He may think, *She's turned into such
a bitch, where can I go to escape this nagging* ... He may conjure up various negative
images of her, seeing the worst in her. She
may think, *What a selfish jerk I married, he
was so understanding and sweet during our
courtship, and now all he does is think of
himself* ... She will start seeing the worst
in him.

While he is at work and she goes about
her daily activities, small matters grow into *monsters* in her mind. By the time the man
comes home after having had his *space* away
from his wife all day long, he is ready for
a little love. Only, she isn't. She feels
and acts negative about everything and he
doesn't know why she is cross with him. The
vicious cycle continues.

In Eileen and Matthew's house it usually goes like this: "You want to be lovey-
dovey when I've struggled with these kids
all day ... my nerves can't take any more
... that includes you." "What did I do?", is
the reply. "Don't give me that. You know
what's wrong with this relationship, only
you don't want to admit it. You want everything to be on your terms and I'm just the
maid around here." This often starts a full-
blown argument, leaving in its wake two unhappy parents and two bewildered children.

The Silent Type and the Chatterbox

Relating - or talking about feelings,
just expressing what comes to mind - can be
a big problem for some men. Most females are

natural chatterboxes, so they usually do not have problems relating.

Although there are many female non-relaters in this world, men usually have more problems in that respect. As in the problems with affection, a man may be the best husband, father, provider and a great lover, but he may have little to converse about. Some partners just do not possess good communication skills. Others -- both male and female -- may simply use their lack (or perceived lack) of communication skills as another weapon in the power struggle between male and female. By withholding their thoughts and feelings, refusing to share them as is to be expected in an intimate relationship, they feel a certain amount of power over their partner. Thus the non-relater can register another *win* in the power struggle.

The partner of a non-relater may feel that he just doesn't have enough confidence in her, that he doesn't trust her with his feelings. It is important for partners of non-relaters to know that their mate's silence is not their fault, but they should not withdraw into their own shell. It is better to continue sharing, showing love and affection, hoping and praying that things will change. Because, if the partners drift too far apart, the marriage may die.

If you are married to a non-relater, in other words, if your partner never talks about anything but trivialities, keeping the *inner sanctum* tightly sealed at all times, discussing the possibility of counseling would be a positive step. Under the guidance of an impartial professional, the non-relater could learn to relax, trust, and feel less vulnerable.

Such a step could greatly improve marital intimacy, and give peace of mind to the partner who has been feeling *left out* for so long. It could also prolong the life of the non-relater, by preventing stress-related illnesses, especially heart disease.

Seeking counseling is easier said than done, since many people - especially men - refuse to see a counselor. If your mate will not see a counselor with you, go by yourself. A good counselor will teach you many ways to handle and cope with a non-relater, and with this new learning, you may eventually convince your partner to go with you.

The Bradshaws, former neighbors of mine, put this into practice. In their case it was the man who was the outgoing type while the wife was extremely moody and withdrawn. So Mr. Bradshaw took the initiative to find a counselor. And since his wife refused to go with him, he went alone. What this husband learned in the sessions with the counselor helped him to better cope with his wife's moodiness, and eventually he was able to convince her to go along. Slowly but surely their relationship improved.

The Emancipated Woman

Modern times have made it necessary for women to cultivate more of the so-called male traits. The modern woman has more responsibilities than women had in the past.

The working woman necessarily needs to put her flexibility to work and exhibit more of the left-brain traits, in other words, more logical thinking, than her more protected mother and grandmother did. She has to make more decisions, especially if she is a single mother. If she is married, some of these changing trends may also intensify the power struggle. On the other hand, the fact that she accepts more responsibilities than women in the past did, may improve her relationship with her husband.

Once again, many difficulties could be avoided if couples would communicate before the wedding. They should discuss all the variables, especially who is responsible for what in the household, each partner's views on family size and child-raising, and how money will be handled.

As if there weren't enough factors contributing to the male-female power struggle and personality dilemma, here is one more.

The Four Basic Personality Types

You may remember having learned about the four basic personality types - melancholic, choleric, phlegmatic, sanguine - which apply to both male and female. I will mention just a few of the traits attributed to these four basic types. No one possesses all of the traits of one or the other type. Most of us are mixtures. But, if you are a good observer, you can peg people as belonging predominantly to one or the other type.

Following are a few of the basic personality traits:

The **melancholic** is usually an introvert, with a moody, gloomy personality and often pessimistic outlook on life. Melancholics usually are highly creative, and often choose careers in the arts or journalism. They are deep, reflective thinkers but are not talkative. They are loyal to family and friends, but tend to be perfectionistic and critical of the imperfections of others. Melancholics are fearful of what others think of them. Their feelings are easily hurt, and they tend to carry grudges for a long time.

The **choleric** is typically extroverted and competitive, in stress terminology, the typical type A personality. Cholerics are self-starters and make great organizers. They are confident and usually bursting with energy and activity. They like to motivate others, and are often pushy and intolerant of laziness on the part of others. Cholerics set goals and they do not stop until they reach them. They tend to call a problem a challenge, and they usually thrive on opposition. Cholerics are optimistic, fearless and bold, and not easily discouraged. With these characteristics, they tend to dominate wherever they go.

The **phlegmatic** tends to be introverted, passive and easy-going. Phlegmatics can sit and just let things be. Phlegmatics are followers. They do not like to lead. They make good, dependable workers in whatever they do, if there is someone telling them what to do. The phlegmatic is not a self-starter. Phlegmatics lack confidence in themselves. They are pessimistic and fearful. They are typically kind-hearted and peace-loving.

The **sanguine** is very extroverted, outgoing and often charismatic. Of the four basic types, the sanguine has the sweetest, most likeable temperament and personality. Sanguines are warm and lively, and tend to be the life of the party wherever they go. But they often lack in reliability. They tend to be talkative. They smile a lot, make friends easily, but also forget them quickly. They do tend to lack self-control, make impulsive decisions, and are generally disorganized. Sanguines usually want to be in the limelight and talk about themselves a lot.

These are but a few of the basic characteristics of the four personality types. And as mentioned above, no one subscribes to all of them. Most people are mixtures of all four types, with a predominance for one or the other. In a marriage, problems can arise when some of the characteristics clash with each other.

Why Are Personality Differences So Important?

Can you imagine a choleric married to a phlegmatic? I can, but with horror.

I see the choleric partner planning projects and activities, trying to motivate the phlegmatic mate to participate, while the latter is content to sit and do nothing. That could mean utmost frustration and thus stress for the choleric, translating into a high level of stress for the relationship.

Or, picture a sanguine, always in a cheerful mood, always optimistic, always wanting to be with people. Now imagine her, trying to motivate a melancholic mate who wants to sit in the den and read all night, to "lighten up" and go to a party on a moment's notice. Frustrating indeed.

So, it is no surprise that personality differences enter into the marital power struggle. True to their personality type, some partners are more easy going than others. Some are quick-tempered, tending to *fly off the handle* without warning, others may think things through before speaking up.

Communication skills and learning self-control can solve many of these problems. Because, although inheritance explains a portion of human behavior, we should not use it as an excuse for everything we do, or don't do. And this applies especially to our most important relationship, our marriage.

Understanding the fundamental differences between males and females, plus the basic personality types, can help greatly when the special stresses of the different life stages arrive. Some of these stages are _nopause for women, the *empty nest*, the male midlife crisis, and last but not least, the senior years. These difficult life stages will add to any existing problems. In fact, they will magnify problems, if couples are not properly prepared to cope, to make the best of them, and come out winners.

Why Women Sometimes Feel Abandoned

Traditionally, women have made their husband the number one focus of their lives. And this predisposes women to the feeling of abandonment when their needs for closeness are not being met. What is meant here is not physical abandonment, but an emotional distancing that sometimes makes a woman feel abandoned by her husband, even though he may be sitting next to her. Some career-oriented women may differ, but millennia of conditioning cannot be undone in one generation.

Men, on the other hand, are conditioned to be more independent. Their career usually comes first, family second.

We women suffer when our men distance themselves from us. Many take the slightest lack of attention so very seriously.

We need to work at understanding why our men act differently than what we expect at times, and become more self-reliant. Little pep-talks, such as, "No human being has the power to ruin my day, not even the one I love most," can do wonders for a woman's psyche and outlook on life. And if you don't feel like smiling, do it anyway. You will feel better about everything if you smile.

If you try to understand your husband, he will more likely come around to understanding you. If people would habitually put themselves into their partner's shoes, great gains in mutual understanding would be made. Where there's limited mutual understanding, there is also the ever-existing pitfall for both partners, namely, vulnerability to the attentions of a member of the opposite sex. This will be dealt with in more detail in a later chapter.

Nagging

Most men do not know how to tell their partner when they feel smothered. Since it is woman's nature to nurture, she wants the best for her family. She wants all family members to have all the virtues she thinks are necessary for a happy healthy life.

This naturally includes well-behaved, clean children, and a loving husband who gives his wife, the children and his chores around the house all the needed attention. This disposes women to more nagging than men, and they often do not realize they nag. In other words, nagging can be completely unconscious.

Another reason women often become *bossy* is the fact that the house is considered the woman's domain. In most households the woman is expected to do most of the housework. So she may nag if the husband or the children do not respect her efforts at keeping a neat house.

Men nag too, but not as much. Most men pay less attention to the behavior of others and more to their own performance. Men often simply *tune out* their wives' nagging. This means the woman has to repeat everything she says, often raising her voice, until the man finally pays attention. This naturally infuriates women, leading to a considerable amount of resentment.

This resentment may fester inside of a woman for a long time, and without realizing it, she may become increasingly negative and critical in her attitude toward her mate. In response to the change in his wife's personality, the husband may have an affair or walk out someday.

In the case of the Hausers, a couple I knew years ago in Germany, this is what happened. After Hans Hauser walked out on his wife, he told me that he still loved her, but he was just tired of her constant nagging and negative attitude. The man admitted that he had never given a thought to the possibility of sharing the blame with his wife. Through intensive counseling, the Hausers got back together and worked things out.

Or, the wife may enter into an affair out of spite, when a little understanding and affection were all she ever wanted.

Communication could prevent the tragedy of many broken marriages.

Oh, Those Hated Chores

Household chores create another set of problems.

In households where both partners are working outside of the home, chores are usually shared. But men's attitude, even though they help with the chores, often leaves much to be desired. Millennia of conditioning as bread winners, being honored and waited on when they came home, can not be wiped out in one or two generations.

Husbands often display the attitude of "I'm helping you do your chores". Many expect a big 'thank you' for their participation, while no one ever thinks of paying the same courtesy to wives. This builds more resentment in women.

I feel lucky. Richard makes breakfast and helps with other things in the household. But his attitude, too, is that he is helping **me** with **my** chores. I am, of course, grateful and frequently thank him.

But deep inside I think, *Why do I say thank you for things that are part of the teamwork in this household?* This is just my opinion, and not a complaint. I try not to let these things bother me.

If, however, you are bothered, then don't let it fester. Talk about it. State, in a non-confrontational way, how this makes you feel. Keep the communication lines open. Get counseling if necessary.

Accept the Inevitable

To our men I say this. You could make your wives and yourselves happier if you would consider chores a fifty-fifty proposition, whenever that is possible. Fight against any resentment you may feel at the arrangement. Just do it. Consider how much she does. If you lower your *resistance* to things you don't want to do, you will lower your own stresses. Most women do not like house cleaning, either.

If we accept the inevitable with a cheerful heart, we all win. By accepting instead of resisting, we avoid resentment. When left to fester in our subconscious mind, resentment can cause considerable trouble at a later time.

Sex

Another area where couples often differ in their views is sex. During the early years of a marriage, sex is usually very enjoyable for both parties. But later on, difficulties may arise.

In most marriages the man wants more sex, and the woman wants more affection. This too has to do with the differences between males and females, reflecting their basic needs. Males naturally are more quickly aroused than females, while the female needs more lengthy *foreplay*.

Men and women do not reach their sexual peak at the same time. Men generally are believed to reach theirs in their twenties, women in their thirties and forties. There are many variations. Attitude and physical health play a big role.

Then there is the factor of habituation. After a few years of marriage, things may become too routine. Interest may wane on both sides. When this happens, communication, understanding and love are sorely needed, to help the couple rekindle interest in each other.

If things have become a bit "old hat" in your marriage, and you have trouble arousing interest in sex with your partner, try fantasizing about him or her - not someone else - and reminisce how things once were. Ask yourself, "Why should it be different now?" The answer will come to you: Routine, habituation, sometimes even laziness. Don't let laziness win over you. Get some bubble bath and a bottle of champagne, light some candles, put on romantic music, and put yourselves and each other in the mood. Fight routine, be creative. It works wonders.

Ladies, remember this. Sex is closely tied to the male ego. Be *his NUMBER ONE FAN. Be supportive at all times.*

A more thorough discussion of this immensely exciting subject is beyond the scope of this book. One thing everyone should keep in mind, namely, education. The more you know about a subject, the better equipped you are to handle problems should they arise. For those who need more knowledge in this area, many books are available.

What Partners Can Do to Achieve Improvement

A wife should learn to recognize that, when her husband acts grumpy or gets angry at little things, he may be experiencing stresses he can not talk about. Instead of showing hurt or hostility, give him *space*.

Because, if you don't, he may retreat further. If you just ignore his behavior as he probably wants you to do, he will soon *bounce back*. Don't perceive your husband's behavior as a personal attack on you. It can not hurt you if you don't let it.

A husband should introspect a little, become aware of his need for distance, then try to communicate this need. He could say, "I really need to be alone right now," rather than *fly off the handle* at some small matter or even push her away if she wants to be affectionate.

He should recognize that his wife may be afraid of losing the closeness she so cherishes. He should watch in her for the signs of this feeling. For instance, she may become highly emotional about an otherwise unimportant issue, or she may ask anxiously, "Do you love me?" Please take her feelings seriously, don't brush them off as childish.

Speaking from experience, once, when I got real *clutchy*, Richard said, "I love you, I appreciate you, but I simply don't want to be with you 24 hours a day." I was hurt, of course, but Richard's comment gave me new insight into his feelings. And I thought, *I don't want to be with you 24 hours a day, either. I enjoy my own company too.*

Why should I take one little comment so seriously? After all, I have worked all my life on bettering myself, on being a complete person whose life is enhanced but not dominated by those I love. But I am also aware of my own tendency to be possessive.

I am married to a man who is not that way. A man who lets me be myself, who has never inhibited me in my quest for self-actualization, for improvement as a person. Richard has supported me in regard to my career, myriad other endeavors, including my often dangerous wilderness adventures with my sled dog team. So, I need to keep telling myself that I owe this same courtesy to him. Namely, to support him in his endeavors and to give him space when he needs it.

Being close, but still functioning as individuals is part of the beauty of marriage.

- The joining together as soulmates.
- Of supporting and loving, of sharing without possessing.
- Of being there when needed.
- Of respecting our differences -- both the basic ones that exist between males and females, and the individual ones, such as personality type, likes and dislikes, and temperament.

So, try to put yourself into your partner's shoes. Sense how he or she feels, then show some understanding and acceptance. Keep reminding yourself of the differences discussed in this chapter.

Don't blame each other for the conditioning we all received during our childhood, plus our inherited traits. Think about these differences, and talk about them in a non-confrontational way. They make good, endless conversation.

Much unhappiness can be avoided if **the communication lines are kept open and the different needs of the partners are met.** Each will be grateful to the other, and neither will feel a need for understanding outside of the marriage. Our soulmates should be our best friends.

CHAPTER II

COMMUNICATION IN MARRIAGE

It has been said that a relationship is only as good as its communication. Thus, it goes without saying that the success of a marriage may well hinge on the communication skills of the partners. The fifty percent divorce rate confirms this.

Lack of communication is one of the most frequent causes of marital strife. If the partners do not learn how to communicate and work out problems or misunderstandings, they can very easily slip into an affair ("He or she understands me,") and ultimately divorce.

This sad truth was once again confirmed to me only a few weeks ago, when a couple I have considered good friends for almost two decades broke up. Kate and Paul were married 35 years and facing retirement from their jobs. This was supposed to be their happy time, the time to do things together, and to relax and enjoy. But it wasn't to be.

One day recently, Paul announced to his wife that he was leaving. He gave no special reason, except, that he had been unhappy in the marriage for a long time. Kate could not believe what she was hearing, and many bitter exchanges and accusations followed. Paul packed his things and left. A devastated wife had to accept the fact that her marriage was over.

According to Kate, she and Paul had not communicated much over the years beyond the subjects of the kids, the household, the weather, and their jobs. But she was content thinking, *when we retire we'll catch up on all that.*

Something Kate said keeps *haunting me:* "If I had only *read* him better." This statement ... if she had only *read* her husband better ... seems to *say it all.* Of course, there was another woman. Did she "read" him better?

When people first fall in love, there never seems to be a problem with communication. We look into our lover's eyes and instinctively know what to do and say, to make him or her happy. We feel so close that words do not even matter at times. When we talk, the flow of words comes easy. We are on a journey of discovering each other, and everything we discover is wonderful, as if viewed through rose-colored glasses. We do not question anything. We see only the best in each other.

With the passage of time, however, the story changes. After people have lived together for some time, the "blinders" of new love come off, and the partners begin to see each other's faults. Or, they disagree on different issues, and either they begin to fight senselessly, or they say nothing and think the irritant or the problem will go away.

Both approaches are wrong. Senseless fighting leads to resentment and more fighting. Maintaining the *status quo* leads to wrong expectations hence resentment, or a broken home. How can one partner know what the other wants if the expectation is not put into words? Why do we expect our partners to be mind-readers? How often have we all heard, or said, "I thought you knew?..."

The above is so clearly shown in Paul and Kate's case. For years, Paul wanted to use all of his vacation days to travel. Kate was a *homebody*. He begged her to go with him, while she frequently encouraged him to travel by himself. I remember once, saying to Kate, "Paul is a good looking man, aren't you worried someone out there might get interested in him?" The reply was so confident, "That's the last thing I worry about." I thought, *What wonderful trust, but I surely wouldn't put it to the test too much if I were Kate.*

Instead of seeking a solution to their differences, especially when it came to Paul's passion for seeing the world, he decided to maintain the *status quo* and travel alone. That seemed acceptable to both, until Paul met someone who shared his love for travel.

If expectations are not met, misunderstandings and disappointments will accumulate over time. After much fighting, one or both partners sometimes withdraw "into their little shell," and this signals the end of marital communication. The partners simply *give up. They may then look for confidants* elsewhere, and if the confidant is a member of the opposite sex, this can be dangerous for the marriage.

Bitterness and resentment resulting from the breakdown of marital communications will grow like a cancer over years, and, if the damage is not repaired, the marriage may die a slow death from neglect.

Don't Wait Until Trouble Starts

Don't wait for trouble caused by misunderstandings and wrong expectations to start, and then look for a quick fix. As in health care, prevention is a lot cheaper and less painful than the cure.

How can trouble be prevented? The

KEEP THE FLAME ALIVE

answer is communication and openness about
feelings before they explode. Storing bad
feelings until there is no more room to keep
them is sometimes referred to as "gunny-
sacking". Then all of a sudden everything
comes out at once due to some tiny "trig-
ger", usually at the wrong time, and defi-
nitely in the wrong form.

A marketing principle comes to mind
here. In marketing, you study the people you
want to serve, their personality, their
needs, then you respond to those factors by
offering what the customer needs or wants.
You can do the same in a relationship. How?

By being aware. Awareness of your partner's facial expressions and body language
will tell you a lot about his or her needs.
Yes, body language, because it is believed
to make up a great portion of human communications.

Then, if something seems amiss other
than a brief grumpy spell, open the communication lines. Try to find out what is going on. If you find out what is bothering
your partner, you can offer to help "repair"
the problem, or apologize if you did or said
something hurtful.

You may say, "I do look at my mate all
the time". If you are a newlywed, you probably do. However, in all but the most ex-
ceptional relationships, the gazing will
diminish with time. Quite often a man does
not remember what his wife's eye color is
because he hasn't looked into her eyes in
years. Or, a wife doesn't notice her husband's new hair cut or a new tie until he
points it out.

Communication and openness seem so
easy in the beginning. But when the excitement of mutual discovery is over, intimacy
decreases, and the partners often lose interest in each other. After a few years of

sharing a home, couples settle down to the daily routines of balancing the budget, taking care of growing children or aging parents, and worrying about career advancement. Their life together as a couple is taken for granted.

Children need all the love and attention we are able to give, but while lavishing love on the children, partners should not forget about each other. In fact, soulmates should come first, children second.

Love is a self-renewing process, the more love you give, the more love grows inside of you. There is enough love in all of us to go around, we do not have to skimp at all.

What's love got to do with marital communication? Everything. Love means caring, and if you care, you will want to know how your partner feels. This means you have to show interest and pay attention, which in turn means you communicate. You find out what your partner's needs are and how you can meet them. If we let love dominate our thoughts, communicating comes more naturally.

The art of communication needs to be nurtured from the beginning of a relationship. Don't stop talking to each other. I mean, the way you used to, about plans for the future, about dreams, not just about business and chores and kids.

Couples should not take the ease of communication and intimacy of the early years of their marriage for granted. As the saying goes, *if you don't use it, you lose it.*

Keep Talking, Keep Sharing

If you don't continue talking to each other, you may end up like so many couples who have told me, "When we are done talking about the kids, we have nothing left to say to each other," or, "We traveled together in the car all the way from Missouri with barely a word spoken." There was nostalgia written all over these people when they told me this, and I would guess that they thought about the old days when they used to sit and talk for hours, and never run out of things to talk about.

So try, try, even if you don't feel like talking. Show interest in your partner, the way you did in the beginning. Eye contact is very important. We are all preoccupied with whatever goes on in our own minds. If you make the effort to have eye contact when your mate speaks to you or when you speak to him or her, instead of looking in a different direction, you show that you are interested, that you are concerned about your mate's welfare, not just your own. If you do this, chances are, your partner will do the same.

We reap what we sow. So when you feel that you and your partner are out of touch, and you feel an emotional distance developing, make filling this gap an immediate priority, and start talking. Talk about your day, how you are feeling at this moment, whatever comes to mind. Don't hold back because you have nothing "important" to say. Your feelings are very important. Sharing in this manner will make you feel connected again.

If the communications gap between you and your partner is big already, don't wait for him or her to try and fill it. Take the first step now. Someone has to, before it's too late. Tell your partner that you feel you are out of touch with each other, and perhaps you can agree on a few minutes every day for a little talk.

Don't hold back on touchy topics, either. They must be discussed, because they won't go away by themselves. Don't think this will be easy. So create a friendly and comfortable atmosphere first, have the coffee ready, or champagne if that's what you both like, then ease into the subject. Begin to talk about your own feelings first. It will get easier once you start.

A word of warning. Keep criticism to yourself for the time. It makes your partner uncomfortable and may drive him or her right back into the little "shell." It is especially important for a woman to make a man feel adequate. Males seem to thrive on encouragement, even more than we females do. So hold the criticism and notice only the things he does right.

Sharing feelings is usually more difficult for men, so give your husband time, lots of time. Since most females tend to be natural "chatterboxes", sharing feelings is much easier for us.

If there are children, of course you will want to include them in all family activities and discussions. But don't forget that parents need to get away from their children too. So take time to be alone regularly, just the two of you. Getting away is especially important if the two of you need to have a long talk. Leave interferences behind and get into the appropriate place and frame of mind.

Some Never Learned How

For many people communicating presents a dilemma. They never learned how. The inability to communicate properly is a product of modern times, and it begins in childhood. In the old days, children used to play, talk a lot, especially about their hopes and

KEEP THE FLAME ALIVE

dreams, make things together, make up all
kinds of games. Now there is television.
Babies are plopped in front of the set, and
that's where some stay glued until the day
they die.

Most people take a short time off their
TV watching habit to flirt, court and marry,
then return to the *tube*. Where are the communication skills? They never learned them.
After all, if people have been entertained
all their lives, why make the effort to communicate now? It is not easy, and it is not
their fault because they were brought up
that way.

Fortunately, parents are becoming increasingly aware of this, and many families
now "ration" TV time and take more time to
talk with their children. Hopefully, the
generation that is growing up now will learn
to communicate again, which will translate
into better relationships in the future.

But the generation now struggling in
their relationships is all too often over-
whelmed by misunderstandings, boredom, disappointment, feelings of emptiness. These
factors often lead to marital infidelity.
The couples of this generation need all the
help they can get.

If help had been available to Penny and
Mike - perhaps in the form of counseling or
books such as the one you are reading now -
they might still be together.

For 10 years after their frairytale
wedding, Penny and Mike seemed to lead *the
ideal life*. Good jobs, lots of travel, and
all the other amenities of a prosperous
life.

Penny had been dreaming about a family
for years, but put off talking about it. She
assumed that Mike felt the same way she did.
After all, doesn't *everybody* want kids? So,

when she felt the time was right for some family planning, she announced that she was ready for a baby. But that wasn't Mike's thought at all. His highest priorities were job advancement, more money, and more fun. This did not include the *inconvenience* of having children around.

Mike did not want to argue, so he evaded the issue. Prolonged, uncomfortable silences followed. Finally, neither partner could stand the stress of these silences any longer. Senseless arguments about other matters followed. The arguments always ended up in another silence phase. There seemed to be no way out of the dilemma.

To make matters worse, Penny "endured" pressure from her parents, who wanted a grandchild. But she did not tell her parents what was going on in her marriage.

Penny's desire to have a baby became overwhelming, to the point where it became an obsession. Yet she did not dare become pregnant without Mike's consent. Without proper communication, the partners drifted further and further apart. The marriage ended in divorce.

Had this couple learned to communicate their wishes and dreams and needs from the start, instead of engaging in a 10-year social whirl before "waking up" to real life, their marriage would probably be blooming now, perhaps with two nice children to be proud of.

Couples need to return to their initial openness. Make at least some time every day to talk with your partner, without interference, without television.

And if you have forgotten how to talk to each other, hurry to a good counselor who can teach you. Or attend a *Marriage Encounter* workshop where couples learn to relate to each other (most churches have information on these workshops). Other options may be short-term couples counseling or a support group.

If you can not convince your partner, get counseling yourself. What you learn may be enough for both of you.

Learn Before You Say "I Do"

As for those now ready to enter into a relationship or marriage, this is where the learning should start. Learn about love, understanding and forgiveness at the beginning. Not the romantic love we all are smitten by initially - that comes all by itself - but the giving kind of love, real love.

Do not ask, "What will I get out of this relationship?" but "What will I bring to it?" If you enter the relationship merely with the thought of having your needs met, forget it. It will not work. Don't expect the relationship to be an instant fix for all your problems. But rather, try to solve your problems before going to the altar. Real happiness does not come instantly, but only through hard work.

If there are unresolved issues and you think, *I'll work on that after the wedding,* don't expect a successful outcome. Talk openly about these things before. If the problem can not be solved before the wedding, it may never be solved.

New problems will surface when two people live together, so don't bring old problems to the union before it starts. It is usually better to part company than to think you will work out problems after the wedding. Otherwise, you may soon end up in a heartbreaking divorce.

Ten years ago Ida, a 38-year-old distant cousin of mine in Germany, married a man the same age, who was very attached to his mother. The mother and son shared a large house. When Manfred, the son, and Ida set their wedding date, the mother assumed that all three could share the big house, at least for a while. But the bride-to-be did not agree. On the advice of her own mother, however, she thought it was better to discuss the matter after the wedding.

After returning from their honeymoon, the new bride told her mother-in-law she now had to move out. Lots of tears and turmoil and strife followed. After several days and nights of arguing, the new bride persuaded her husband to move his mother into an apartment. That was that.

But the pain will always be remembered, and the resentment will probably never go away. Clear communication before the wedding could have made things much easier.

As I already mentioned, talk comes easy during our initial discovery stage, but we often tend to embellish things. It is important to talk openly with your partner about your hopes and dreams and plans for the future. Don't hold back on the not so wonderful aspects of yourself. Be frank about things from your past that your partner should know. Do seek professional advice on "touchy" topics if necessary.

A couple I have known for many years recently broke up, supposedly because of something in the past of the woman, something her husband felt she should have told him. I don't know any other details about this story, and perhaps the event that occurred in the past was only one of many problems. In any case, the past did haunt the marriage, and, after 18 years and three children, it died.

KEEP THE FLAME ALIVE

Bottom Line

Learn to communicate before the wedding day. Talk clearly about your expectations and ask your partner about his. Make sure you understand each other fully. Don't forget to establish clear guidelines on finances, the division of household chores, and family planning.

If you are not sure you understood a statement correctly, ask your partner to repeat it. If you have not learned how to talk and argue properly and intelligently, without hurting feelings, seek out a counselor to give you a brief set of instructions, or turn to the books and tapes listed in the references at the end of this book.

Pointers For All Couples

Here are a few pointers for all couples, young and old. There is never a need or justification to hurt each other's feelings. Never say "You always do such and such," but instead, say "I feel such and such about a certain matter, it hurts me when... ".

For example, if your husband leaves the dining room right after dinner and heads for his easy chair in front of the television set, you could say in a nice tone, "Honey, I don't mind your watching television after dinner, but it would be nice if you would at least help me clear the table. If you just walk out of the room it makes me feel like I'm only the maid around here."

Stating **how you feel** takes the *sting* out of your words. In other words, you do not judge your partner. You merely state how your mate's behavior or a certain situation makes **you** feel.

The non-combative, non-confrontational approach may not always work well if one or both partners are grumpy or tired. Recently Richard and I returned from a long car trip to another state, only to find out that our house sitter never showed up to stay at our home while we were gone.

I was upset and wanted to call the woman right away. Richard said, "Don't say anything, there is nothing we can do about it now." He was right. I pointed out that I was not going to be nasty, just tell her that I was very disappointed. He got upset with me and said I should not.

In that case, we were both "edgy" because we were tired, and this could have exploded into an unnecessary argument had I pursued the matter at that time. So I decided to say no more about it. Needless to say, one must be extra careful at times like that.

If you have to fight about something, hold your temper, listen to what your partner says, then reply. Don't interrupt. I know this is much easier said than done, but if you work on your communication skills and have some consideration for each other's opinions, you can handle the argument in a more dignified manner. This makes all the difference in the world.

You may not reach an understanding, but if at least you haven't hurled nasty words at each other, there won't be so much resentment buried in the unconscious mind where it will cause trouble later on. You could hug and make up, and say, "We must talk about this some more." Then set time aside to continue. But do remember to settle the matter soon or reach a compromise. The status quo will blow up at you later.

This dignified approach is not easy for people with a quick temper. But it is your responsibility to work on controlling your temper if you want to avoid hurting your partner's feelings. Respect those feelings. Don't label them as silly or dumb, and don't interrupt. Listen! Listen! Listen!

The inherent differences between people do make for different fighting styles. Some must get the grievance out immediately or they will explode, and if they get it off their chest, they feel better and are ready to make up.

Others avoid an argument at any cost, just keeping all complaints to themselves. This type of partner heads for trouble, and so does the marriage. If this person continues to refuse to communicate, to relate, to discuss an important issue, he or she may accumulate grievances for years, until a breaking point is reached. And when this point is reached, it could manifest itself in a physical or mental breakdown or both, or a breakup of the marriage.

If you have a partner who refuses to relate, who simply keeps all of his hopes, dreams, problems, joys and sorrows locked up inside, I hope you can find a way to *draw this person out*, or your marriage may eventually erode. Those of you who have this trait, I beg you, if you love your mate, help him or her to understand you. Your mate can not do this if you refuse to communicate. Your partner will be happy and grateful if you show some confidence, show that you trust her or him with your feelings.

Why do People Withdraw?

I wonder why people roll themselves up into a cocoon after the initial openness? Did something happen to drive the person into a shell? Or is this partner returning to his or her true personality type after the *adrenalin rush* of young love has passed?

Perhaps personality, heredity and one's upbringing predispose to this unwillingness to communicate or to learn to communicate. But we can all learn. It is a matter of attitude, of realizing that we can all improve our lives if we just soften up to see the other side of the coin, to loosen up the old resistance, to give and take.

The Moody Partner

And what about the partner who controls the other with moodiness? Yes this is a form of control, because it can keep the other partner in a state of constant tension, never knowing when the next *funk* will come.

Moodiness may be part of a *melancholic* personality as explained in Chapter I. It may be due to a person's heredity, premenstrual tension in females, depression, and myriad other reasons. But it can also be due to lack of consideration for the other's feelings. Because, the other partner may worry that she or he did or said something inappropriate or hurtful, something that upset the moody one. If the moody person doesn't communicate, how can the other apologize if an apology is in order?

Long ago in Germany I knew a woman who *controlled* her husband and son and daughter with her gloomy moods. Evie, her daughter, who was a close friend of mine, told me that these moods came on very suddenly, and that they sometimes lasted for days. Sometimes Hilda, the mother, would put a scrumptious meal on the table, then suddenly her facial expression would take on a *martyr's* look, and she would disappear into the bedroom without saying a word. (Was it because compliments didn't come soon enough)?

The whole family would then rush to her side to inquire what was wrong. Usually there was no response from the *pouting* mom. But the meal was always ruined.

After this woman's husband died, her moods got worse. Every time the now grown children went somewhere without asking her to come along, the martyr expression and silence would take over. Evie finally moved away, but the son, Gunter, still dutifully visits mother every day, waiting on her, enduring her moods.

Bottom line. Old Hilda, now in her upper eighties, will probably continue to control her son with her moods. Needless to say what this is doing to the man's relationship with his wife.

I appeal to all you moody people, try to be open about what is bothering you. This can make such a difference in your relationships. If you just want to be left alone to think out a problem, say so. Your partner will feel better and give you the space you need.

If you live with a moody person, it is necessary for you to become emotionally hardened to the moods. But this is difficult for some, and you may lie awake wondering why your partner doesn't love you enough to trust you with his or her feelings. If these episodes repeat themselves often, communication, in general, will continue to deteriorate. Sometimes the non-moody partner may give up and stop trying. This could eventually spell doom for the marriage.

If you already know that your partner just needs a little *space* temporarily, then you have probably learned to live with this. If not, pouring your heart out to a trusted friend, clergy person or counselor may be what you need to help you cope with the situation.

It is difficult to live with a moody person, but you don't have to let it destroy your relationship. If you can manage not to let the moods affect your state of mind, and simply wait patiently until they end, that's fine. But if the moods bother you, perhaps you can try to discuss the bad moods when your partner is in a good mood. Although you will be so happy when the bad mood is over, that you don't want to bring it up, don't be lulled into complacency, because the *demons* will strike again. You may want to bring it out in the open before that happens. You can tell your partner that you love him or her and that you want to help, but that you feel *shut out*.

Although withdrawing is more of a male than a female trait, general moodiness affects both sexes. If you have established through communication that your partner just wants space and that there is nothing else wrong, then you can ignore the moods and go about your own projects cheerfully. Work on yourself so it won't affect your emotions and personality. Perceive the moods as your partner's problem and don't let them control your mind. Because, after some time, your partner's moods may *rub off* on your own state of mind.

If you live with a sourpuss day after day, year after year, it may eventually take a toll on your personality. Resentment for all the times your partner ruined the good mood you were in, buried inside you perhaps for years, may eventually sour your attitude toward your mate, and life in general.

This could create a vicious cycle that may be impossible to break. It goes like this. Suddenly your partner, who has been taking your cheerful nature for granted, will start seeing the sourpuss in you, and what he sees he will not like. Of course the original sourpuss will not admit that he or she brought on your sour attitude.

If you as a couple have not communicated in years, your partner will probably be totally oblivious to the situation, seeing only what he or she doesn't like in you. Since you have grown more negative in your attitude toward your mate, you, in turn, will start seeing the worst in him or her. Frictions over little things will become routine in the household, and your opinions of each other will worsen. Of course, when you expect the worst, you get the worst, hence you will continue to bring out the worst in each other. You may still love each other, but since your love is not getting the nourishment it needs, it will die. Divorce court may be the next stage.

But the above scenario need not happen. There is still time to reverse this terrible situation. Finding a good counselor should be the first step. For those who have faith in God, lots of prayer has been known to be successful in patching up *needy* relationships. But it is a two-way street. One partner can not do it alone.

Acceptance

Effective communication and open relating are great builders of marital intimacy. In fact, I can not imagine how a relationship could possibly succeed without these attributes.

But what if you can not bring your mate out of his or her silence, even with counseling? Then it will be time to assess your feelings. Ask yourself:

- *How much does it bother me?*
- *Can I live a happy life without communication?*
- *Is my partner loving and generally*

wonderful in every other respect?
- Do we at least communicate non-verbally, i.e, hold hands frequently?
- Do I feel connected to my mate when we hold hands, or re-connected if there was an argument, or an apology was made?
If the answers to the above questions are "yes", then, hopefully, you can work on acceptance. Employ a counselor if you need help. Or perhaps you can talk to your clergy person. Ask him or her to join you in prayer for the strength to cope. That is, if you have faith in God. As mentioned above, prayer can be a powerful help.
Don't force the issue any longer. Just be there for your partner. Be patient and loving, while attending to your own agenda and taking care of yourself.

As already mentioned, we can not change people, only ourselves. So, working on your own attitude - changing it from a critical one to an accepting one - is all you can do if you want to save your marriage. That's all any of us can do, and must do if we want to live life to its fullest.

Conflicts and Hard Times

Crises and conflicts will arise in every marriage. If you learn to communicate before troubles come your way, coping will be easier. This is especially important during illness, letting go of grown children (the empty nest), the female menopause with its physical disturbances and emotional upheavals, or the famous male midlife crisis, during which men frequently become depressed.

Partners may become irritable and angry during these stages, and these emotions in turn can exert powerful negative effects on one's surroundings, especially one's mate.

Last but not least, the frailties of old age will be easier to handle with good communication skills. Partners will be able to give each other the needed support during this perhaps most difficult stage of life, if they have learned to communicate in appropriate, loving ways.

We all have different coping styles, and many people sail right through these difficult stages gracefully, often without taking notice of the stresses involved. Others have endless troubles. A later chapter will deal in more detail with stress and methods of coping. In brief, staying aware and keeping the communication lines open, will make any crisis situation easier to deal with. So, don't ever stop relating!

Humor

Humor is another great *icebreaker* and enhancer of marital communications and intimacy. In *Proverbs,* the Bible states, "A cheerful heart is good medicine, but a crushed spirit dries up the bones" (Prov. 17:22).

We need to laugh often, even - or especially - at ourselves. When you and your partner laugh together, you renew the bond between you. Laughter makes us momentarily feel carefree.

Remember how you felt when you were courting, all the silly things you did together, like tickling, chasing each other around the house, playing like little children. If you do not find anything to laugh about, think of something that happened in the past, smile about that event (... feel good already ? ...) giggle, laugh out loud. Try it, and let yourself feel good. Share these thoughts with your partner. Look at old photo albums or videos together, especially funny ones. Old pictures and memories strengthen bonds between people.

Tell a good joke once in a while, or often. If you - like myself - don't remember jokes well, write them down. In fact, keep a *joy list*, writing down funny things that happened in the past, then pull them out when you need a laugh. Share it with your mate.

I decided to do this several years ago, writing down only the funniest things. The list has grown to more than 30 items, some of them I remembered from way back. One even goes back to my childhood. I had forgotten it, and suddenly it came back to my mind.

I was 10 years old. My mother and I stayed at a relative's house overnight, and we shared a bed. In a dream I was having a fight with my girl friend. I rose to my knees, slapped my poor sleeping mother in the face and then proceeded to beat on her with my fists. I did not wake up until she grabbed me by the shoulders and shook me, asking, "What are you doing?"

I laughed so hard remembering this episode, tears streamed down my face. I hurried and added it to the list right then and there, so I would not forget it, ever.

Many other items are on that list. Some are funny only to me. Some are quite embarrassing. Some were not so funny when they happened, but now I can have a good laugh about them.

Feedback, Compliments, and Working Things Out

Part of the art of communication is feedback. We need to let each other know how we are doing, how we are feeling about life in general, on a daily basis. This goes a long way toward keeping us from engaging in self-destructive behavior. It keeps the spirit healthy.

Be *upbeat* and complimentary toward your partner. A little flattery is OK, but not too much, or it becomes *phony*. Remember that honesty is the biggest cornerstone of a good marriage.

If you have a fight, do it fairly and constructively, as previously described. Dissonance occurs in every relationship. We all get angry at each other. Working things out by using communication skills rather than letting blind rage take over is a *must*.

If you *keep your cool,* you will learn where you stand with each other. This will keep you from making wrong assumptions and having wrong expectations. If you refrain from hurting each other's feelings and work things out peaceably, you will get your harmony back, even enhance it.

A later chapter will deal more in depth with resolving conflict and forgiving. It will teach you how to get harmony back into your relationship, by forgiving, by *wiping the slate clean*, so you can have a new beginning.

Last But Not Least

Good communication would not be complete without saying "I LOVE YOU" often. This is harder for some people than for others. If those three magic words were not used routinely in your family, it will be more difficult for you to say them. But do try. Your mate needs this reassurance often, and so do you.

CHAPTER III

COMMITMENT - THE STUFF CHARACTER IS MADE OF

I recently heard a story in which a lady was asked on her 60th wedding anniversary, whether she had ever considered divorcing her husband during all those years of their marriage. Somewhat indignant about the question, she said, "Kill him?, yes, but divorce him?, no." Does that sound like old fashioned commitment?

My mother, now 86 years old, pounded into my head hundreds, maybe thousands of times, that "You must do what you promised to do, even *if it kills you*, and you must finish what you start, even if you don't want to."

These are the "old-fashioned" values I grew up with. Do any of our young people know what this means? It means **commitment.** These values mold you into a reliable person, one who does not go back on his or her word, one who keeps promises.

Why is Everyone so Afraid of Commitment These Days?

We enter into marriage promising to love one another for better or for worse. Yet when we arrive at our first hurdle, that vow seems all but forgotten. Things are no longer comfortable, no longer convenient. We want out.

The time we live in could be called the "Me First" era. The modern mindset calls for individualism, independence and personal freedom. Not that there is anything wrong with those, if we don't forget our commitments.

Unfortunately, many people don't want to give, just take. "Me first," screams the inner voice. This is not to say that we should deprive ourselves of the good things life has to offer. On the contrary, we should love ourselves enough to take care of ourselves, and at the same time give our love freely to others, especially our soulmates and children.

People do not seem to realize that, the more love we give, the more love is returned to us. But we are afraid to love. We fear that, if we do too much giving and loving, we will be considered weak and oldfashioned.

People are busy doing the things they consider important. Often they just do not want to take the time to nurture a relationship and keep promises. It's too much trouble. It is easier to get out, enjoy freedom once again.

Why, then, did we give up our precious freedom in the first place? Because we were lonely. We knew that, no matter how well life was going, no matter how many of the good things in life we already had, there was an empty space within us, and that empty space yearned to be filled. We yearned for love, to care for another person, to share, to relate, to become one with another.

So we went - no, we rushed - to the altar and said, "I do." Then, when the initial blaze had burned out and a little trouble came in, it was easier to run than to work things out.

It is human nature to want the easy way out of any situation. But that is why we learn (or at least are supposed to learn) self-discipline when we are young. If we have self-discipline, we act like human beings, using common sense in our decisions.

We do not act like animals, who follow only their basic instincts.

The Basic Premise of Marriage

Let's go back to the basic premise of marriage. To say our marriage vows does not mean we are going to have fun and games forever. It is far more serious. When we say "I do," we make a commitment, a solemn promise that is meant to last a lifetime... **'til death do us part'**.

Marital commitment needs to be stronger now than in the old days. Why? Because there are more forces out there, trying to destroy marriages. Television is one of them.

With near-naked bodies, immoral *bedroom scenes, adultery, and the bad guy* often going unpunished, many programs seem specifically designed to undermine morals.

Subliminally, if we keep watching them, these programs affect all of us. And subliminally they can erode our marriages over time, if we let them. "So, what do I watch if there is nothing else on?" you may say. How about public television or a good book? By-product: Improvement of the brain.

As I mentioned above, when I was a child, I was taught that a promise means you keep the promise no matter what. Promises were kept, for better or for worse. And *for worse* comes in every marriage at some time or another. We are human beings, and human beings make mistakes.

Add to that illnesses, accidents, and the frailties and disabilities of old age, and you will find out that something beyond the starry-eyed dreams and promise that we will *love each other forever* is needed.

Promises

Children should be taught to think about a promise before they make it. In other words, teach them not to commit themselves until they are sure they will be able to take the consequences of the commitment. This will help shape their character and prevent many mistakes.

If children are not taught that it is wrong to break a promise, then they will develop into unreliable adults. People who can never be trusted, people who make promises but keep them only if they feel like doing so. People who have no self-discipline when it comes to keeping a promise - both within and outside of their marriage. We all know them. People without commitment, without loyalty. They just follow - to state it in Freudian terms - the id.

The id is the child inside of all of us, demanding immediate gratification at any particular moment, regardless of the consequences, regardless of promises made to the contrary, regardless of the hurt this may cause.

If I have just painted a dismal picture of irresponsibility, of lack of commitment, this is nevertheless a way of life for many. And sadly, this irresponsibility spills over into the relationships of such people. They never learned in their childhood what commitment means, so how could they be responsible adults and act appropriately?

I'll Try It, and If I Don't Like It, I'll Leave

Many people enter into marriage not with the thought of sharing the rest of their days with their mate, but with the thought, *I'll try marriage, if I don't get what I expect out of it, I'll just leave.*

Parents should do all they can to prevent the lack of commitment which ultimately causes such an irresponsible attitude toward the sacred institution of marriage. How? By being good role models. By showing love and loyalty to each other, by being faithful, by being committed.

Stay Committed to Marriage Vows

During our wedding ceremony Richard and I took two candles, lit one candle together, then blew out the two. This is a common ritual.

I wonder though, how many people think of its meaning. Couples would do well to remind themselves frequently of the significance of such a beautiful ritual, actually its frightening significance.

Because, when lighting the single candle and blowing out the two individual candles, you have made the biggest commitment of your life, that of dedicating your life to another person. If couples would contemplate this commitment more often, they would take better care to nurture the relationship.

If married partners would remind themselves from time to time of the promises they made during their wedding ceremony, they would be less reluctant to standing by each other, instead of running at the first sign of trouble.

So why not get your wedding pictures out once in a while and look at them together, as a *support* for fading memories. Then reaffirm: "I'm committed to you no matter what the future brings!"

A word of warning here. If you are searching for ways to enhance commitment in your marriage, don't do it by having more children. Years ago, a neighbor of mine, Marie, thought she could accomplish this.

Marie's husband, Todd, was a good man, but he seemed more committed to his passion of jumping out of airplanes than to his wife and two small girls. And on non-flying week-ends, he would pack parachutes for others (he was the club's "expert" at that chore). So even if it rained or snowed, Todd rarely spent a whole weekend with his family.

I was raising my little boy at that time, so Marie and I did some "coffee-klatching" now and then, comparing notes about kids, etc. Marie complained bitterly about her situation, and one day she said, "If I had another baby, Todd would surely stay home."

I told her I would not count on it, but she went ahead and got pregnant anyway. Not because she wanted a third child, but be-cause she thought this would increase her husband's commitment to his family.

So, Marie had another baby girl. It looked as though her little "scheme" had worked. For about three weeks, anyway. Then Todd went back to his jumping and packing routine. But - you guessed it - Marie did not learn anything.

This woman tried the routine one more time, by having a fourth child, a boy this time. And - you guessed it again - it didn't work any better than before. You may have guessed this one too - Marie and Todd got a divorce two years after their fourth child.

Almost a *carbon copy* of this story happened to another couple I knew some time ago. And it ended the same way as Marie and Todd's, after baby number four.

When Peter and Shirley were married, Peter had dreams of a great social life and the lure of foreign countries, with one or two children added sometime in the future. Shirley had dreams of a big family, not sometime in the future, but right away. So, the babies started coming. One every year. Naturally, there was no time and no money for vacations.

While Peter sat on their porch on warm summer evenings playing his guitar and singing songs, Shirley prepared baby bottles and changed diapers.

And the separate dreams and lives of Peter and Shirley continued, with little communication between them. Peter did not pay much attention to his children. As time went by, the partners had less and less to say to each other.

I remember Shirley telling me that after each child Peter was helpful around the house and his attitude toward her and the children *improved* somewhat. But soon he would withdraw into his *little shell* again. Was she contemplating her fifth child? I'll never know. She didn't have a chance. In Shirley's own words, "After taking such good care of me for two weeks after I came home from the hospital with little Mikie, Peter packed his bags and left."

I'm not passing judgment on this husband's lack of commitment, the wife's wrong approach to getting it, and the lack of communication between those two people. I'm only confirming what I said above. If you want more commitment, having more kids is not the way to get it.

Married People Live Longer Than Singles

I will now appeal to your selfishness. Those who may believe that all the talk about holy matrimony is just sentimentality, and that we really don't need each other, should acquaint themselves with a wealth of psychological - and more recently medical - research.

These findings demonstrate that love and intimacy are necessary for a satisfying life, and that they contribute not only to mental but also to physical well-being. In fact, epidemiological studies (conducted over large timespans) show that married people enjoy greater longevity than unmarried folks.

Standing by Your Partner has Many Rewards

Although emotional detachment is often described as a way to avoid the pain of loss, it is far better to commit to another human being, because the joy received from the companionship far outweighs the hurt that close ties with another human being may sometimes bring.

If we grow and mature together, and nurture our relationships, we will be ready to weather the storms. When we promise *for better or for worse,* we need to realize that, as already mentioned, *for worse* will come.

Marriage is a two-way street. In our characteristic human selfishness we may be afraid that we will have to "give" a little extra. We need to realize that, if we *walk the extra mile* for our partner, he or she will return the favor when the need for extra support arises. There may be exceptions, but a *giver* tends to bring out that good trait in others.

Commitment in marriage means that we keep our bargains. The returns can be multifold. If we are ready and braced for the storms, such as sickness and other crises, they will not destroy us. If we think in terms of commitment rather than selfish pursuits, we will build our emotional hardiness

60

and character strength, so we can pass the tests that will come.

The story of actor Christopher Reeves, who became a quadriplegic as a result of a horseback riding accident he had in the summer of 1995, comes to mind. One of the most shining examples of marital commitment is the devoted support Dana Reeves has been giving her husband since the accident.

In an interview with Barbara Walters (20/20, September 29, 1995), Dana said it has all been a test of her marriage vows. This fine woman obviously considers all she does for her paralyzed husband just a "labor of love," keeping the promise she made when she said, "I do." The love and gratitude she receives in return is overwhelming.

Sexual Commitment

Commitment and loyalty to one's spouse will grow, steadily decrease, or die completely, depending on the kind of nurturing or lack of nurturing the relationship gets from the partners. This includes **complete fidelity!**

It goes without saying that we should not nourish sexual fantasies about anyone outside of the marriage. Why? Because we are all human, and we must control our minds in order to be able to control our bodies. If you want to stay sexually committed to your partner, then simply stay out of danger. There will be more on this subject in later chapters.

Be Each Other's Best Friend

In committing ourselves to another person, we should automatically be each other's best friends, always keeping our partner's best interests in mind, taking care to meet

KEEP THE FLAME ALIVE

each other's needs, and accepting the other as he or she is.

About Those Needs

As mentioned in Chapter II, meeting your partner's needs means first learning what these needs are. And, since many of these needs are quite different for males and females, we must make a firm commitment to better understand one another and our different needs.

Last But Not Least

Keep loving. Jesus commanded us to love one another. Love can never deplete itself. The more it is expressed, the more it grows. In giving love, we gain more and more of it. Isn't that worth a little commitment?

CHAPTER IV

EXPECTATIONS

Through life, we fulfill many self-fulfilling prophecies, or expectancies, most of which we are not even aware of. The child who eavesdrops on a conversation during which he is described as not very bright will unconsciously fulfill this prophecy throughout life. That is, unless he later recognizes what is happening - perhaps through a good mentor - and decides to actively work on the problem and change it.

So it is with a bright child who hears that she is bright but not very good at math. All through life she may excel at everything else, but always with the thought that she is not good at math. This could build into a fear of math so strong, that it may keep this child from choosing a dreamed-of career in science.

I Want My Children to be Perfect

The child who is brought up with the belief that he must be perfect at every-thing he does, will try to fulfill this ex-pectancy through life. This child will do his best, but after realizing that he can not be perfect, he may grow up never be-lieving in himself, always thinking that his performance is not good enough.

Unreasonable expectancies can create low self-esteem. People with a low self-concept - although this occurs on an uncon-scious level, are continually telling them-selves, "I'm not worthy."

They can not accept their own imperfections, and thus they seem to be unable to love themselves as they should. Since we must first be able to love ourselves before we can love others, low self-esteem can have adverse effects on relationships. It would be wise for parents to consider this when raising children.

Unreasonable Expectations

The unreasonable expectancies built into people during childhood, can have many other adverse consequences throughout life. For instance, such people are often approval seekers in everything they do. Approval seekers don't trust their own judgment without the approval of others. They often lack enough confidence in themselves to stand by their decisions. The ultimate consequence is that approval seekers give others too much power over them.

When applied to our relationships, the families we grow up in exert a greater influence than most of us realize. Perhaps mostly on a subconscious level, our parents practically imprint on our psyches what kind of relationships we should have, what traits to look for in a mate, etc. So, many self-fulfilling prophecies are created during our childhood, and we spend much of our life fulfilling them, being burdened by them, or successfully or unsuccessfully fighting them.

Unconscious Forces at Work

It is believed that there are deep, powerful, unconscious forces at work in all of us, which attract us to the partners we eventually end up marrying. The "programming" we received during childhood draws us, almost by a hypnotic force, toward the person we want to spend the rest of our life with. Something in that person *connects* us to parts of our own beings, and this initiates the *bonding*. Those who claim that they have experienced *love at first sight* feel this more strongly than others.

But the emotional *templates* our families have stamped on our psyches often interfere with what we, on the conscious level, expect to give to and receive from our partners. Struggles and conflicts keep surfacing during our relationships, confusing what we expect and what our upbringing tells us to expect from our partners. If we do not work through these emotions and put communication skills to work, sending CLEAR SIGNALS, this can wreak havoc in our relationships.

A sad story comes to mind here, the story of a couple that should have stayed happily married. But sadly, they recently divorced. Too many confusing signals were sent and received, spelling doom for the marriage.

Ron and Jill had, what I thought was the ideal relationship. Ron had brought two young children to the marriage. Jill wanted children of her own, but could not have children. While being a good wife and a wonderful mother to her stepchildren, Jill never completely lost her desire to have a baby of her own. In fact, the desire to have a child cast some dark shadows on the marriage on and off over the years, and these intensified after the *nest became empty*.

Jill - although she needed her husband more than ever during this time - acted out against him. She generally made Ron feel as though he was not important to her, that she only cared about the children. In truth, Jill loved her husband very much, but let her *obsession* with having children get in the way of expressing her love for him. She sent all the wrong signals.

Ron often felt rejected by his wife. Eventually he *went astray*, and the marriage ended. Because of other circumstances, reconciliation can never occur. Ron and Jill are still friends. According to Ron, "the feeling, on both sides, will never go away." What a tragedy. All that love, lost forever.

We Often Get What We Expect

In her book, *You Can Heal Your Life,* author Louise Hay claims that we are one hundred percent responsible for everything that happens to us, including illness. Though I do not completely share her opinion (children and animals do not expect to get sick), I feel that there is a lot of truth to it. For example, if you expect to get a lot of colds, you will get a lot of colds.

In our relationships, if our expectations are good ones, we will most likely receive good things. But if, for instance, we suffer from low self esteem, our inner voice may tell us, *I'm not worthy.* Our partners will *pick up* on this, and may agree with our low expectation. In other words, low expectations, low yield.

Body Language

Body Language is a powerful communicator. We have all heard it said that a certain person COMMANDS respect. Translated to relationships, this means that if you expect to be treated in a certain way, you will usually get that treatment. In other words, if you expect to be respected and act in respectable ways, your mate will respect you.

As already mentioned, sometimes we send conflicting signals to our partners. For example, the mouth may smile, but the eyes do not. The mouth may say one thing, but body language says the opposite. Quite often, body language wins.

This means that, consciously or unconsciously, people send out signals about their expectations, and how they feel about each other. It is good to be aware of this, and take care not to send the wrong signals. As in Jill and Ron's case, wrong signals led to a tragic divorce.

Fear May Draw Dreaded Experience To You

Sometimes the things we fear the most are the things that will happen to us. It is believed that fearful thoughts can be energized by our fears, and thus we could draw the frightening experience to us.

In relating this theory to marriage, if you fear that your partner will leave you or do other things that make you unhappy, this is more likely to happen than if you have confidence in your partner's loyalty and commitment to you.

It can even happen in violence situations. If the husband of a battered wife promises he'll never beat her again, she does, of course, want to believe him. On the conscious level she may try hard to believe this promise, but deep inside there is always the fear of it happening again. This translates to a subconscious expectancy, and sooner or later it will happen again, until this woman decides to break the ties of the relationship.

I knew several women who endured the horror of sharing their life with a wife beater. These women lived in constant fear, yet they kept trying to believe the promises that *it won't happen again*. In each instance the vicious cycle was not broken until the woman walked out.

My first husband, Bill, was a temper loser who would *fly into a rage, smashing* up things around the house. The episodes came in response to minor triggers such as not being able to reach someone by phone. He never beat me, and I was confident that he never would, because he respected me *very much*. After his tantrums Bill always apologized, and I always tried to believe him when he said this was the last of the tantrums. My body language probably *gave away* my subconscious fear of the next episode. The tantrums continued, and he refused to get therapy for his problem. The episodes of rage increased in frequency and intensity. After seven years of living in fear - and expectation - of the next tantrum, it became clear to me that a divorce was my only choice.

Following are more examples of wrong expectations:

If you suspect your partner of being unfaithful, your anxiety will manifest in your body language, even if you do not actually speak of your fears. This will tell your partner that this is what you expect.

Your partner's unconscious mind may say, *If I have the name, I might as well have the game*. No one would ever admit to such thinking. However, unless that partner has an exceptionally strong will and high moral standards, the expectation will be fulfilled when the opportunity presents itself.

If you think of your partner as quite a charmer, a natural flirt, this expectation too will be answered. Your partner will charm you, and others.

If your partner tends to drink too much, you will most likely expect this behavior to be repeated (we all base our expectations on *track records*), and if the vicious cycle is not broken, it will continue.

If your partner feels you will scold him for coming home late, as has been happening in the past, he will probably act out that expectation with strong body language. In response to this body language, you will feel compelled to meet the expectation, even though your mind may have been made up not to say anything. Suddenly, as if pushed by an invisible force, you blurt out, "You're late again." Your partner, in turn, will say to himself, *See, I knew she'd criticize me, she always does*. And so the vicious cycle of expectations and fulfilling them goes on.

The Vicious Cycle Continues

Telling lies is another example. If a child tells a lie and gets caught and punished, he or she may lie again and again, out of fear. The child lies in order to avoid the unpleasant consequence of his or her actions (expectation), and the vicious cycle continues.

The same can occur in a marriage. For example, a partner knows unpleasant things will happen if a *misdeed* is discovered (expectation), so he or she works hard at covering it up. The vicious cycle of lies and coverup and more lies is hard to break, so it goes without saying that partners should accept that *honesty is a must!*

Thoughts Control Behavior

We can break the vicious cycles of expectations and their fulfillment, by controlling our thoughts. If we short-circuit negative thoughts when they occur, the inappropriate expectations will not be expressed in our body language. If our body language does not express them, our partner's subconscious mind won't sense them.

How can I short-circuit inappropriate thoughts when they come to mind? Many methods of doing this have been proposed.

Here are some of them:

- Just say - out loud if you wish - "STOP!".

- Distract yourself. Remember how you sometimes stop a young child's undesirable behavior by distracting her rather than by punishment. The same goes for your own inappropriate thoughts. So, take a deep breath and think of something pleasant and positive, like your last or next vacation, or something funny that happened to you or someone you know. If this is difficult, force yourself.

Remember, you control your thoughts! If we control our fearful thoughts, our feelings will follow suit. Sometimes it may help to briefly acknowledge an undesirable thought, then *let it go*.

Many books, especially those on stress control, deal with these things in detail. These books - available at libraries and book stores - can teach you step by step how to do it. Also remember that there is a virtual army of counselors out there, ready to help you, your clergy person included. Last but not least, don't forget prayer.

For those who have faith, prayer can be the most powerful aid to changing negative thoughts into positive thoughts, negative expectations into positive ones. Note: If you want to pray but don't know how, ask your clergy person to help you.

I Wish My Mate Would Change

During courtship we often think of the other's potential and what we will do with that potential. Consciously or unconsciously, we may think of what we will do to change certain things that do not quite fill our expectations.

One partner usually does not realize that the other thinks along the same lines. If things are not what you expect from your partner before the wedding, they will be much more difficult to deal with after. As mentioned in the chapter on communications, for a relationship to be rewarding and lasting, expectations must be discussed before the wedding.

When couples talk of their hopes and dreams for a life together, they should also include the less romantic parts of their expectations, such as the division of household chores and money management. Talking with your chosen one about your needs and expectations before the wedding will give you a good idea of the prospects of having these needs filled. It will prevent a lot of nagging and bickering in the future. And, it is absolutely necessary that partners be honest in discussing their needs, especially emotional ones. Subtle body language signals will tell if a person is sincere when promising to meet these expectations.

What If Expectations Were Not Discussed Before The Wedding

If people do not see eye to eye on important things before the wedding, chances are that this won't change much after the knot is tied.

What do you do if none of these things were set straight beforehand, as so often

happens? Then you may just have to change
some of your own expectations, and try to
love your partner into coming around to filling at least some of them. This is easier
said than done, of course.

A word of warning here. Nagging has
never changed anyone, so resist the temptation, watch your words. Clear communication is a must. Get counseling in how to
handle the situation. Stick with love. It is
the force that works miracles.

My Own Story Of Change

Now I will bare my soul to my readers.
Several years ago I attended an excellent
sermon given in connection with a Bible
Study session. Following some of the advice
given in this sermon changed my marriage.
Actually, it changed me first.

Richard and I had, what we thought, a
good marriage. But for years a few things
had been missing. There was a decrease of
affection, lack of mutual awareness, lack of
physical contact and lack of *spiritual* con-
nectedness. We were busy, so we didn't pay
much attention to our needs, in fact, we
paid little attention to one another in
those days. But ignoring needs never makes
them go away.

The sermon was about relationships, and
I can still hear the lady minister's voice
in my ear: "You want your partner to change?
No, YOU CHANGE!" These words changed my
life. Instead of resenting Richard for not
hugging me enough but being too proud to hug
him first, I just gave myself a push and did
it, again and again and again. Persistence
worked. We now touch and hold hands whenever
we can, including in public.

Julia's Story

Julia, an acquaintance, told me her story of misguided expectations, and the tragedy they created. She discovered that her husband of 25 years had a deep friendship with a woman at his office.

Julia - although she believed her husband when he told her that sex was not involved - suffered deeply at what she considered his betrayal. To make matters worse, her husband said he never loved her (his wife) in the first place. The shock was enormous. Julia couldn't sleep and couldn't concentrate on her work. The thought that her husband betrayed her (if only platonically) and that he never loved her tortured her day and night, and her health deteriorated.

After talking to a counselor, Julia began to dig into her own psyche in an attempt to find answers. She found that she put out the wrong signals throughout the years of her marriage. She never let her man know what she really expected from him, namely, love and commitment. Julia was a humble person who never asked anything for herself, especially not of her husband. She did not even realize consciously that she deserved better than what she received from him. What she received was all the material things a wife could want, but practically no attention from her man.

The other woman, on the other hand, begged for attention eight hours of every day in the office, and she finally received it. The wife just didn't try hard enough, and the husband thought she cared only about the nice things he provided for her and expected nothing else.

Without communication between these two partners, the husband's mind had become somewhat *twisted*. He later admitted that he was all mixed up in his feelings and thought he never really loved his wife. Actually, because of his response to the attentions of the other woman, and the infatuation he developed for her, he rationalized his feelings into thinking that he never loved his wife anyway. It made him feel less guilty. By allowing wrong thinking to control him, he almost lost his wife.

This story had a happy ending. The couple worked things out. The husband voluntarily changed jobs to make parting with his friend easier. Husband and wife saw a counselor for several months, and also attended a *Marriage Encounter* session.

They are now happier than they ever were. They accepted the pain as a growth experience. Both changed their ways, and made their expectations known more clearly.

Moral of These Stories

Ladies, if you want your husbands to be more loving, more affectionate, put your pride aside, and JUST DO IT! By hugging frequently, without accusing him of not returning the hugs at first, you will communicate your expectation, and in due time he will catch on and enjoy it.

There are, of course, exceptions to every rule, but in a high percentage of relationships, this method will work. If the husband happens to the affectionate one and the wife isn't, then I say again, JUST DO IT!

Show Each Other Confidence, Appreciation, and Admiration

Confidence in good, desirable things is the expectation we need to nourish. This means you should hold your partner in high regard. If you disrespect him or her, your body language will tell.

We all have the need to be appreciated. The more appreciation you show, the more you will get in return.

You may say, "But I have lost respect for my mate." Do some soul searching within yourself to determine if you love your partner enough to make the effort to regain the lost respect? Remember, love is a choice, and so is respect. Search for the traits you loved and respected at the beginning of your relationship.

Perhaps you did not show enough appreciation of the good traits, and perhaps you did not indicate that you expected those good traits to continue to shine throughout the years. You may need counseling to accomplish all this, to help you determine the right course to follow on the road to regaining the respect, appreciation and admiration you once had for him or her.

And, if things have happened that led to loss of respect and confidence in your mate, then I remind you that we are all human, we all make mistakes. The loss of feelings need not be final. Many things can be rectified if we develop tolerance for the flaws of others, and can find it in our hearts to forgive mistakes that were made.

If you decide you want to somehow regain your respect for your partner, then start concentrating on his or her good qualities. Everyone has some. Single them out and show appreciation and admiration for these good qualities, and you will see small miracles every day.

By recognizing your partner's good traits and paying them compliments, while ignoring the undesirable ones, chances are that he or she will be eager to multiply the good traits. Because, it feels good to be appreciated.

We all need appreciation, and we need admiration too. We all have something to give that deserves admiration. Look for it in your mate. You will find it!

As Phil, a happily married friend of mine once said: "You want to know what keeps a man at home? Simple: EGO STROKES." We all need them, but men are especially needy in that regard.

And, there is one other need men have, but rarely voice. *A good looking wife.* This does not mean you have to be a beauty queen, you just have to take care of what you have. It means, clean hair, neatly kept clothes (spots and wrinkles are really disturbing). Last but not least, keep your weight under control, especially if he is thin. The extra effort to look as good as you can, *for him,* shows your man that you respect him enough to make that effort. He will feel honored.

These things are so simple, one wonders why they are so often forgotten. We all need to be appreciated. We all need admiration. We all need those strokes, in fact, we crave them. Why, then, are we often so reluctant to give them?

Positive Expectations Work Best

Although some situations seem hopeless, positive expectations are much more likely to lead to positive results, while negative expectations will always get you negative results. In other words, if you want your relationship to flourish, positive expectations are the way to start.

It should be understood, of course, that expectations must be realistic. They should be in line with your partner's capabilities. If expectations are too high, you set yourself up for disappointments.

Realize That Not Every Trait Will Change

Some things in a person must be accepted as they are. No one is perfect. If you love your partner enough, then accept him or her, and apply the expectation to yourself, to improving your own attitude toward your partner, to coping, and forgiving if there is something to forgive.

Help your partner with her or his problems, but do not let these problems ruin your life. Be committed to your own happiness and make the best of your relationship.

Make A List

If your relationship no longer fills your expectations, it may be helpful to make a list of your partner's good and less desirable traits and idiosyncrasies, then see which portion of the list is the longest. Are the good points worth staying (happily) together?

If the answer is *yes*, keep sending out positive signals. Do not look at what has been lost or was never there, and be grateful for the good things that are there at this moment.

We are all responsible for our own happiness. We should, of course, expect our partners to add to this happiness, but we should never expect them to be totally responsible for it. We should never rely on any human being to make us happy, only on ourselves. That's one expectation we alone have the power to fulfill. Let's all do it!

CHAPTER V

THE GRASS IS ALWAYS GREENER ON THE OTHER SIDE

Yes, that's how the old saying goes ... *the grass is always greener on the other side of the fence* .... But you know what, it's just as hard to cut.

Nevertheless, it is in the nature of cows, horses, and other herbivores, to think that the grass from which they are separated by a fence is better than the grass that is freely available to them. This same urge exists in humans. If we can have it freely, it is not as attractive as if there is a barrier between IT - whatever or whoever IT is, and us. Since, however, people are supposed to have more common sense than horses and cows, we must also know that this is nothing but an illusion.

Those who habitually go after the presumably greener grass can attest to this. The moment they taste this presumably greener grass, it is no better than the grass they ate before they made that great effort to climb the barrier. So they abandon it and climb another barrier, and another, and another, only to be disappointed again, and again, and again.

Eventually, at least one hopes, these fence climbers will learn that when they get there, "THERE" will just become another "HERE". So why waste the effort?

You think your mate just doesn't live up to your expectations, and you want to take the easy way out instead of working out your problems. Now, do you really think the next one, the one that looks so good on the other side of the barrier to be climbed, will be better?

Don't be naive. There is a high probability that the answer to that is no. Because, if you are not able to work things out with the one you thought was perfect for you when you said "I do," then, the next one will very likely be a disappointment too. Or, if you find your partner boring compared to the way he or she was in the beginning, maybe you are the bore, maybe you should do something to become more exciting yourself. The excitement in a relationship will continue if the partners work at it, and nourish that flame so it won't go out.

So don't be a fool. Don't throw away years of shared dreams and the history you built together, just to *try the grass on the other side of the fence*. The fun will be short-lived, and then it will turn sour. The brief adrenalin boost you may get from that fence-climbing effort may also ruin several lives. Is finding out if the grass is really greener on the other side worth this?

If you already jumped, you may say, "I just wanted to have a little fun, break the monotony. It meant nothing." Do you know what it meant to your partner? Do you know that your brief romp on the other side of the fence may have caused more pain than you could ever imagine? Do you also know that, regardless of how carefully you cleared that fence and returned to your own pasture, your partner felt that you had been on the other side?

If your partner felt it, he or she may suffer in silence and never ask you about your "adventure." But it is very likely that your little adventure marked the beginning of the erosion of your marriage. The guilt you carry around will make things between you and your partner even worse.

There will be an unspoken "something" in the air, an uneasiness you both feel, and it will not get better by itself. You and your mate will drift further and further apart. If that is not what you want, then watch your thoughts and actions carefully next time you see an opportunity to stray. Yes your thoughts, because that's where the trouble starts. If you think positively about your mate and your relationship, you will be happy right on your own side of the fence.

Flirting

If you look around, wherever you go, even at the checkouts of the grocery store, the flirters are there. Many of them may be harmless, just passing the time, but not all are. If you hold a flirter's gaze, you may have just made a dangerous contact if you are married. If you hold that gaze a second too long, this will very likely be perceived by the stranger as a sign of interest on your part. If you do not want it to go any further, look away and don't look back.

If you need to confirm in your mind that you are still attractive to the opposite sex, consider this brief eye contact as a small ego booster - God knows we all need them - but stop right there. Smile to yourself and go on.

I was brought up to look away if a member of the opposite sex looks at me with interest. Times are not that strict any more, and one could be considered an *oddball* if one holds to those old fashioned manners. Perhaps a *middle of the road approach* could be found for modern behavior, interesting enough to maintain a spark between the sexes, but without sending signals that could cause trouble.

My Flirting Test

As a scientist, I recently felt the urge to conduct my own little *flirting test* on a plane returning from Europe. I stood up, facing the other passengers, and gazed at some of the men, to see if they would respond. Then, when a man returned my gaze, I looked away. I repeated the action once or twice, then never looked back. The experi-*ment* was concluded. Results: I got favo-rable responses from several handsome men, none from others. I assume the latter were the faithful ones.

These men must have thought I was com-ing on to them, and I applaud those who did not return my *overture. One of them, I later found out, was a Baptist minister on a trip home to the US from his missionary work in Africa. Incidentally,* my self-concept re-mained intact despite the "rejects."

Beware of Parties and the Work Place

Parties, especially office parties, are dangerous flirting grounds. But the work place, club, even meetings, can be just as dangerous. At parties, a few drinks may loosen people up enough to become reckless and flirt intensely, even if they would never do this in the sober state. Regret-table mistakes are easy to make at times like that.

A friend recently told me that her son, now married three years, had resisted the office Christmas party (without partners) and several other informal after-work get-togethers before Christmas. This young man had once been "famous" in his own circles for cheating on every steady girl friend he ever had. When the surprised mother asked her son what changed, he said "why look for the opportunity?". My friend, whose husband left her for another woman several years ago, said she was very proud of her son.

Opportunity is the key word there. Many good people go astray because of opportunity. If the moth keeps hanging around the flame, it will eventually get too close and burn!

It starts harmless, but beware, it will not stay that way. If you think it will spice up your marriage to make your partner a little jealous, don't do it! As mentioned above, be especially wary of eye contact. Bonding to a stranger can begin within seconds. You gaze into a stranger's eyes and suddenly you feel you know this person. A very powerful, very dangerous cluster of feelings may begin at that precise moment, and this can have marked adverse effects even on a solid relationship.

In the work place, people frequently work so closely together that it is almost inevitable to get to know each other well. Actually, you do not get to know your associates. You get to know only what they want you to know - their best side. So you may fantasize, and think, *if my wife or husband would treat me as nicely* ... I suggest you stop the musing right there. Don't be fooled. Very likely, your associate is as bored at home as you are, and doesn't treat his or her partner any different than you treat yours.

And, if you two are about to start an office affair, thinking, *Oh, but we are so right for each-other* ... that too is a fantasy which will wear off. When you live with a person, you will get to know that person's down side too. And we all have one of those. *For better or for worse* includes each partner's down side, the good and the less desirable traits. That's why people

should get to know each-other well before
tying the knot. Be sure that you can accept
ALL traits, not only the wonderful ones.

Fantasies

Fantasizing has been touted by some as
"good for your marriage." Perhaps fantasizing about a movie star you'll never meet in
person isn't that bad. But if you catch
yourself fantasizing about someone you see
often, a red flag should go up in your
consciousness.

It is human nature to fantasize, but
before you allow yourself to daydream about
someone other than your marriage partner,
try this. Fantasize about your own. Just let
your mind drift back to your wedding day and
other joyful occasions. You'll find a whole
new world of enjoyment.

**Things You Can Do to Keep the Grass Green on
Your Side**

Try a little understanding of your
mate's shortcomings and problems. Because,
if you don't, someone else will. Or, that
person will pretend to.

For those who think they need the
"stimulant" of a new association to "boost"
excitement in their marriage, there is a
better way. Explore what it is that you find
missing, the void you are so desperately
trying to fill by seeing someone else. Then
get counseling and "clean up your own emotional garden" rather than messing up someone else's.

For men who want to turn their lives
and their marriages around, there is an
organization called Promise Keepers. Its
members are committed to spiritual, moral,
ethical and sexual purity. They are dedi-

cated to strong marital and family relationships through love and keeping of the TEN COMMANDMENTS. Members of Promise Keepers help each other to *stay on the right track*.

Most churches can give you more information about Promise Keepers. Their magazine, titled NEW MAN, is listed in the references at the end of this book.

Stop criticizing. Forgive me for bringing this point up often. It is so important I feel I must *hammer it in*, to myself and anyone who will listen. Think of your mate's good traits. As I said in the chapter on expectations. If you expect good things, you have a better chance of getting them. If you expect bad things, you are sure to get them.

If you are harboring resentment toward your mate, it has been suggested that if you act loving you'll feel loving. Acting "as if" is a deliberate effort to change negative thoughts about your partner to loving thoughts. So, even if you can't change your feelings, you can change your behavior. Acting the way you want to feel can make you feel better. Why not try it? What do you have to lose?

Communicate. If you don't know how, learn from a counselor. Staying on the proper side of the fence has a lot to do with meeting needs. If you do not communicate, you may not even realize what most of your mate's needs are, unless you rely on body language. But that could be dangerous because the signals may be confusing, leading to misunderstandings.

So find out what your partner's needs really are, before someone on the other side of the fence does. Because, that may just spell doom for your marriage.

If your partner did jump that fence, do not retaliate by doing the same. Two wrongs do not make a right. Forgiveness is the only way. The alternative is bitterness, which will destroy your life. It will even take a toll on your looks and your health. Forgiveness will be dealt with in a later chapter.

Last but not least, work hard at enhancing your mate's self-concept. Remember, those who get their ego strokes in their own pasture have no need to try the grass on the other side.

Sisters, You Hold the Key

Part of today's epidemic of adultery and divorce lies in the hands of the ladies. Men have always thought of themselves as the hunters, but nowadays they quite often are the prey. Many women have taken up *the sport* too, and some go quite aggressively after their *prey*, married or not.

Some may say, *times have changed,* and that this author is just old-fashioned. But, have our feelings changed too? Does it hurt less than in the old days if you are on the receiving end of the infidelity?

The saying goes: *Do onto others as you want others to do onto you.* Or, one could say, *Don't do onto others as you don't want them to do onto you.*

"Someone took my husband, and now I'll take someone else's." Each time I hear that kind of statement - sometimes from a friend - I feel terribly disturbed. I point out that hurting someone else will just cause more pain. It won't take away the hurt suffered, but it will establish a never-ending vicious cycle.

Often the reply is: "I don't care." How dreadfully wrong! Why hurt someone innocent? Doesn't the woman who is about to enter into an affair with a married man realize that the man she pries away from his wife may be taken away from her by some other *predator* out for prey? If this man could be pried away from his wife once, there is a strong likelihood that he will *fall* again. IT'S A MATTER OF CHARACTER!

Some say, "Oh, but it's different with us, he'll be faithful to ME, because he really loves ME" ... History speaks for itself! The Bible says, *we reap what we sow*. And what those who take someone else's mate sow is the beginning of another vicious cycle of pain and more pain.

And the cycle won't end until you women out there start seeing the light, realize that you are bringing disaster on yourself and others.

Yes, ladies, it's in your hands! When you start saying NO to the urge to take someone else's man, this vicious cycle, and with it the epidemic of marital infidelity and divorce, will stop. The healing can begin for all.

So, girls, how about sticking together from now on, and make this world a better place for ourselves and our children. Let's return to the old-fashioned morals most of us grew up with, and stop the divorce epidemic *dead in its tracks*. How about it? Are you with me on this? I hope so.

Why Did Women Change So Much?

I believe it has to do with "feeling their oats".. Women have been "suppressed" - or at least that's how many perceived it - for millennia. But now we girls feel strong, invincible. Much resentment against the male of the species, *Mister Macho*, has built up in our psyches over millennia. It is coming out in many ways, and one of these ways is to control men for a change, as they have controlled us throughout history.

But You Are Going About it The Wrong Way, Ladies

Wouldn't it be better for women to stick together to attain their goals in life, rather than hurt other women in the process? Besides, you are not controlling men that way, you are just making it easier for them to get all the free sex they want.

Men don't have to look for sex anymore. It is offered to them wherever they go. I wonder what this is doing to the *"business"* of prostitution? Because, "nice girls" are doing it for free.

Men may regret that the challenge of the chase is gone, but many enjoy the ego trip. Others have told me that they are turned off by women's promiscuity and would rather be in charge of the *mating scene*. In other words, men would like to make their own choices, and in the end, most men prefer women who are not boldly pursuing them. And they certainly have no respect for those who do. So, maybe the old fashioned game of "playing hard to get" is better after all.

Men, Beware of Unexpected Emotions

A one-night stand or occasional "get-together" outside of his marriage usually means nothing to a man. However, sometimes even men - women too, but I'm focusing on men now - get tangled in some unexpected emotions. Like addicts, they may say "I can take it or leave it, I have it all under control." It usually doesn't work that way. The affair that was initially meant to be just an occasional *diversion*, may "grow on them". Before they know it they may find themselves in divorce court. Many regret it by then, and wish they could undo what happened.

According to statistics, a man rarely marries the female who was instrumental in breaking up his marriage. So the man who went too far often loses his family, ruining his and several other lives in the process. He ends up all alone, having to prove himself all over again and try to rebuild his life. The *aftershocks* of divorce and the guilt feelings may wreak havoc with his life for years to come.

Sexually Transmitted Diseases and Other Health Problems

Consider the physical consequences of adultery for a moment. It only takes one time to get AIDS, genital herpes, gonorrhea or any other sexually transmitted disease. This applies to both sexes. How devastating for the partner who thought her or his beloved was faithful. No one deserves that!

Several years ago I read about an observational study demonstrating that men who were not faithful to their wives had considerably higher heart attack rates. I don't think a study was needed to determine this.

Jumping fences causes marked physical exertion, and if this jumping is done in an effort to get at the *forbidden fruit*, it causes extreme mental stress as well. It goes without saying that this stress, combined with the guilt feelings for leading a dual life, of covering up with lies and more lies, can have a devastating effect on the health of the individual. And it may just cause that dreaded heart attack.

We Didn't Have Sex, So It Wasn't an Affair

Wow ... wait a minute ... That's what people say when their *platonic* relationships are discovered. Many hurt partners,

both male and female, can attest to the
contrary.

I have talked to numerous people whose
partners had such *platonic friendships*, and
these were so intense that they either destroyed or severely eroded the marriage.

A mother told me about her young single
daughter who had a deep, intimate but not
sexual friendship with a married man. The
young woman always looked forward to being
wined and dined once a week by this well-
to-do older man.

During their *luncheon dates at fancy
restaurants* the man told his young friend
many things about himself, things he claimed
he could not tell his wife. Did he ever try?
Both considered the "affair" harmless. The
girl never knew how their meetings affected
the man's family life, and what havoc their
"friendship" played in this man's marriage.
He never told her of his wife's suspicions,
and how she often tossed and turned all
night because she couldn't sleep. Nor did he
tell her that he covered up his guilt by
making her think she was doing something
wrong in their marriage, not he.

Fortunately, the mother of the young
girl was able to persuade her daughter to
let go of her "sugardaddy" and turn her attention to men her own age. After the girl
said her final farewell to the man, he was
heartbroken and became depressed. His wife
convinced him to see a counselor. Through
counseling, the man learned to relate to his
own wife, and both found new joys in their
marriage. The suffering the *platonic* affair
caused could have been avoided had this man
learned to relate to his wife, instead of
looking for friendship elsewhere.

Similar, sexless affairs are everywhere. They usually consist of clandestine
lunches (we are not having sex, so we don't

owe our partners an explanation), meeting for a drink or coffee after work, a little hand-holding now and then, and the feeling of having "such a wonderful listener, such an understanding friend."

Perhaps those who *sneak around* to find a good friend and listener outside of their marriage would find this friend and listener at home too, if they tried. The person at home most likely feels hurt and left out, and would like a chance to be a friend too. These so-called friendships turn the world of the partner at home upside down. And, although the wrongdoer may cry "nothing happened," for the left-out partner this pla-*tonical relationship* may be just as hard to bear as a full-blown sexual affair. So, to all those who think they are doing nothing wrong, consider the fact that investing time and emotions in a relationship outside of your marriage is not as harmless as you think. Think about the hurt you cause, and the fact that this gratification you are treating yourself to can spell the beginning of the end of your marriage.

And don't say, "I can handle my emotions", because the realization that you have developed feelings for an "understanding" friend may just sneak up on you, and you may be in trouble. In other words, these "dates without sex" may just get you more than you had bargained for: A divorce.

A "let's get together and talk" relationship can go on for years. It may develop into more, it may not. But there's no way around it. If you are honest with your partner and do not keep the meetings a secret, your mate may be jealous and hurt. If you keep them a secret, it is plainly and simply a betrayal of your marriage vows. It is **emotional infidelity**.

THE GRASS IS ALWAYS GREENER...

The Story of the Leaking Faucet

Don't think infidelity isn't possible among the older generation. A minister told this story from the pulpit.

In an apartment house there lives an older widow. She does not have anyone to fix things around the apartment when they break down, and she can not afford an expensive contractor. Quite often she feels disturbed by the realization that she has no one to turn to when she needs help.

So one day, when a faucet is leaking, the widow asks the man next door if he could help. This man, a retiree, lives in this building with his wife. The nice man says "sure, I'll help you out." So he takes his little tool box to the lady's apartment and fixes the faucet.

The lady asks if she can pay him, but he won't accept money. "Oh, how very sweet of you, I'm so grateful ... here, I just made a fresh pot of coffee, have some, and some cookies. I baked them myself this morning." "Sure," says the man, "I'm a big coffee drinker, and chocolate chip cookies are my favorite."

They sit and talk, and the lady just bubbles over with gratitude, telling him again and again what a nice man he is. The man thinks, ... *my wife is never that grateful when I fix things around the house ... why, she doesn't even say thank you ... just takes everything for granted ... and how long has it been since she told me I was nice ...? probably not since our honeymoon, at least I can't remember ...*

He finally returns to his own apartment, still smiling to himself, thinking how refreshing it was to talk with that lady, how good her compliments made him feel.

Next time he walks by the woman's apartment he thinks .... *Wonder if she has another leaking faucet to fix ... ?*

Neat little story. And it has a moral. Be nice to your partner, always be grateful for things he or she does for you, and don't forget the compliments. Don't ever forget to say, "Thank you". And if you tell your man he is wonderful he won't have to wait for the widow next door to satisfy his craving for ego strokes.

Last But Not Least, Beware of the Signs

What signs? Well, they are not universal, but based on conversations with people who had experience, here are a few signs that may mean on-going or impending infidelity. They are, however, not always to be interpreted as that.

They may be flukes, coincidence. So don't take them too seriously. Be as nice as you can be, and keep your eyes open.

- Your partner stays at the office longer than usual.

- Your previously patient partner starts *flying off the handle* frequently, blaming you for everything that goes wrong. This may be a sign of stress due to other reasons, or it could be the stress of a double life.

- Your partner does a lot of "preening", generally worrying more about his or her appearance than before. All of a sudden she worries about the pinch test when she hasn't cared about her weight in years, and suddenly he, the big couch potato, wants to join a health club.

- Sudden changes in food taste. (Who introduced this carnivore to all those vegetarian dishes he shunned before?)

- Distant look, dreamy eyes, a look you haven't seen since your honeymoon.

- A radiant smile when talking to someone at the office on the phone ... people usually don't *radiate* when talking business. Or, that same smile when talking **about** someone at the office.

- Suddenly your partner starts rubbing and caressing you in ways he never did in 20 years of marriage. Though you love it, you wonder where it comes from. And where did we learn that new lovemaking technique? From a book? But where's the book?

These are but a few of the many subtle or not so subtle signs of a change in your partner's life or outlook on life. Generally watch for uncharacteristic gestures and routines, especially in a person who has always been one hundred percent predictable, who has always done things in exactly the same manner.

PLEASE KEEP THIS IN MIND. Don't become paranoid, because these changes may be pure coincidence. Use these signs to probe into what your partner may need and what you are not providing. Look for ways to increase the closeness with your partner.

Bottom Line

Both sexual and sexless extramarital relationships can have powerful adverse effects on all those involved. So, if you really think the grass is greener on the other side of the fence, don't be fooled into thinking that changing partners - be it temporarily or permanently - will be the solution to your yearnings. It never is. Nurturing your own grass is more rewarding.

KEEP THE FLAME ALIVE

And if you need occasional adrenalin rushes, try an exciting sport.

It is safer, won't get you AIDS, and it won't destroy lives.

CHAPTER VI

AFTER THINGS HAVE GONE WRONG

You've discovered that your wife or husband is having, or had, an affair. What now?

Whatever your reaction may be, try to stay calm. Don't do anything rash. At the moment you discover that you have been betrayed, seeking revenge by having an affair of your own may be the thing you find most suitable to soothe your pain.

But "getting back" at the wrongdoer is not the answer. Remember that two wrongs do not make a right. That's easy to say when your own world did not just come to an end. But do know that few people haven't experienced THE PAIN. You will survive.

So, don't stoop to the wrongdoer's level. Keep your pride and save yourself additional emotional "baggage" to carry around for the rest of your life.

In the forgiveness chapter we will deal with this further. For now, let's discuss what happened. You may say to me, "How can you discuss this when you don't even know the circumstances?" You are right. I can only draw on the study of millennia of human experience and what people tell me.

Time Will Heal the Wound

Whether you get a divorce or not, time will heal the wound. The scar tissue, however, will remain, and it will occasionally cause you trouble. In other words, some mental anguish will plague you from time to time. It will lessen over the years, if you do not allow yourself to dwell on it too much. It is best to briefly acknowledge the painful memory when it *plagues* you, then cut it off by forcing yourself to think more pleasant thoughts. If you allow yourself to dwell on it, you will have a lifelong fight against destructive emotions ahead of you. Don't allow these emotions to destroy you.

How can I stop them when they come? By working actively on mechanisms to release the past instead of *holding on* to it. This will be difficult. You will grieve, which is part of the healing process. You need to grieve at first, as you would at the passing of a loved one. You can not rush this process in the beginning, but after some time you can accelerate it by actively working on release mechanisms. Some of these will be described in the chapter on forgiveness. They won't work overnight. For your own sake, give them a try.

When I was young I often studied facial expressions of people. I frequently noticed the bitter facial expressions of middle aged and older women, even if they were laughing or smiling. In my youthful naivety and innocence I thought that these women must have had a hard life. Perhaps they had to work too hard, or they suffered severe illnesses at one time or another. Perhaps some of their children were in trouble.

All of those factors may have applied, but now I am wise enough to know that the bitterness and resentment expressed in these faces more likely had different causes. Nothing can quite compare to the facial expression of a betrayed woman.

Men have better "poker faces." They develop wrinkles, but most of them hide their emotions better. Do they actually suffer less? Not being a man, I can not describe how a man feels. But I believe men suffer just as much as women do when they feel betrayed by one they loved and trusted. I also believe that the level of suffering depends on the individual.

How severely we suffer has much to do with how hardy or tough we are, emotionally. In any case, the pain can be almost unbearable. If the betrayer happens to be the one to whom you dedicated the best years of your life, it is unrealistic to expect the pain to disappear. But, as mentioned above, it will lessen with time, leaving you with a few more wrinkles and an ache in your heart.

Life goes on, and you have no choice but to pull yourself together, to get strong, to think of ways to prevent a recurrence (to be discussed in the last chapter), and to work on forgiveness. This is assuming that the affair has ended.

Partner Refuses to End the Affair

What if the affair is still going on? That is the bitterest of all pills to swallow. You may then need much soul searching and perhaps counseling to help you decide whether you will confront the wrongdoers, wait things out, or walk out. Don't go it alone. Get the help you need. And if you believe in prayer, use this powerful weapon, and ask your friends to pray for you too.

If I were your counselor, I would say, "Don't put up with it for one more minute. Tell your partner that he or she must never see the other man or woman again."

Don't beg and plead. A woman in her mid-forties, whose husband recently left her for another woman, told me how much she cried and pleaded, how she practically got on her knees and begged him to come back to her. This woman did everything she could think of to please the man. She even gave in when he occasionally visited, wanting sex. This did not make him stay. Then she got pastoral counseling, along with the prayer of many people in her church. This turned her life around. She realized that begging and being subservient only made the man turn further away from her. I have a feeling he did not respect that in her.

With the help and support she received, this woman has since *re-invented* herself. She has become stronger and better looking. And she now says "NO" when her husband visits and wants to make love. She is friendly but distant. She believes that her husband respects her more now. The divorce is not final as yet, and she told me she will consider reconciliation if he gives up the other woman.

Lately, the man's visits to their 18-year-old son are becoming more and more frequent. Is this a sign that he is more interested in his wife again, now that she is no longer *begging* him to come back? Time will tell.

You will have to decide on your own behavior towards your mate, whether to be loving and try to salvage things, act indifferent toward her or him, or turn away and end the relationship.

Much depends on what your relationship was like before the disaster struck. Was it a good relationship at one time, but the flame somehow went out? Or was it a lukewarm, mediocre union from the start?

The decision is yours. Do you choose to try to regain the respect you once had for your partner? Or do you despise or even hate him or her, and just want to distance yourself from the relationship?

If, after a confrontation, your partner insists on continuing the affair but does not want to lose his or her family, this

person may need the only "treatment" that
often works for an alcoholic who refuses
rehabilitation. It's called *tough love*.
Namely, to be thrown out into the street.
Some people come around fast when that happens.

Whatever you do, try to keep your dig-
nity. If you have children, consider their
feelings too, and their future. Even teen-
agers and young adults suffer when their
parents go through hard times, or a divorce.
They may act nonchalant about it, but believe me, they suffer. And, statistically,
people from broken marriages are about fifty
percent more likely to get divorced. So,
don't react too fast. Think it through.

What Next?

If the affair has ended, you can have
closure and try to patch things up. Although
it seems impossible not to blame the guilty
party, blaming accomplishes nothing. It will
only breed resentment and resistance to
change in your partner. Because, being reminded of a wrong committed will lead him or
her to defending the wrongdoing.

Besides, if your partner is willing to
give up the alliance with his or her lover
and reconcile, reminding him or her of the
affair is not productive, because you want
your partner to forget the past and look to
the future.

Now is the time to look for things you
yourself may have done to provoke the infidelity. If you made mistakes, do not blame
yourself. Forgive yourself for whatever it
was that you did wrong, and try to do better
in the future. Start on the road to forgiveness. Put yourself in your partner's shoes
and imagine what could have provoked the
situation. Perhaps your partner was lonely

or needed an ego boost at the time you were away on a trip. Perhaps it was a "slipup" and then the other party kept coming on, and your partner was too weak to end the alliance.

That doesn't mean that your partner was justified in having an affair, it only means that human beings are weak. Circumstances and opportunity can sometimes break down even a person with good morals. <u>To err is human!</u>

Lessons Learned

Over the years, Jody and Jim were regarded by their friends as the "ideal couple." They are both self employed, with separate, unrelated businesses. They are beautiful people in their forties. On social occasions, they always acted loving. They were polite and attentive to each other, and it looked as though their 20-year marriage "made in heaven" was meant to remain there. But things are not always what they seem.

Their story, as told me by Jody, goes like this. The marriage was generally the loving union it seemed to be. But over the last few years a little boredom had set in. Jody and Jim took each other more and more for granted, followed their own interests and generally drifted apart.

Ego strokes, which came so easily during the earlier years of their marriage, had all but stopped. No one seemed to miss them in particular. Or did they miss them, but were too busy to be fully aware of this change.

Household routines were normal when both were in town, and there were never any arguments. That should have raised a red flag for both of these two intelligent people. As a psychologist friend of mine once said, "A marriage without fights will eventually die in the mist."

Jim had always leaned toward friendships with women instead of other males; he simply preferred *sisters* instead of *buddies*. Jody thought his close friendship with a female friend (she was a friend of her's too, or so Jody thought) was just filling the void of yearning for the sister he never had. So she did not object to his frequent visits to her house to play "handyman" after she was divorced from her husband.

Jody was never jealous, at least not at first. She went on several short business trips that fateful summer when her world collapsed. Upon her return from one such trip she noticed a big change in Jim's behavior. The sweet, polite man had changed, quite abruptly she thought.

Suddenly he started "acting out." He was crabby, blamed his wife for many small things that went wrong in the household, saw only her worst traits and none of the good ones, and so on. When asked, "What's wrong," the angry reply was always, "Nothing."

At first, Jody thought Jim was just depressed about business not going well, but then she heard that this "sister" he spent so much time with had acquired quite a reputation after her divorce. Rumor had it that she "went after all the married men in her neighborhood". And to make matters even more complicated, she was involved with the husband of Jody's best friend, among others.

Jody, still completely naive, told Jim perhaps he should stop seeing this woman because of her reputation. People might think he is involved too. At that moment, this man, who had never blushed in all the years Jody knew him, turned crimson red in the face. This was the precise moment that Jody realized that Jim <u>was</u> involved. She

now says, "I never knew one's world could
crumble so quickly, it felt as though my
whole life just got blown to pieces with
dynamite."

This story did have a happy ending.
Confronted, Jim denied everything, but later
admitted to a *platonic* involvement. Jody
chose to believe him. He promised not to see
the so-called sister again, even though she
kept calling him to tell him about all her
troubles. But for several more months Jim's
face often had a very said, "whipped puppy"
expression.

Jody forgave, but also accepted part of
the blame for neglecting her husband and
their marriage. Now, years later, Jody tells
me that the acute pain did not even begin to
ease until the end of the first year, even
though their marriage underwent a wonderful
renewal and revival. After two years the
pain was gone, but even now, four years
later, "scar tissue" still causes trouble on
and off.

Moral of the story. Mutual appreciation
had stopped for this couple, ego strokes had
stopped, communication had stopped. And ego
strokes from someone else, plus loneliness
while Jody was on her trips, caused this
good man to "fall", if only *platonically*.
Fortunately, the situation was remedied.

Jody decided to "invest" more time in
her marriage and less time in her business.
She continues to give lots of attention and
ego strokes to her husband, and he does the
same for her. They take in more entertain-
ment, do more things together. The marriage,
according to Jody, is happier than it had
been in years, and she says sometimes she
wants to call the "sister" and tell her
thanks for the *wakeup lesson*.

Another lesson comes from Jim and
Jody's experience. Namely - as already

mentioned - that a platonical relationship can wreak just as much havoc in a marriage as a full-blown sexual affair.

Another couple I know did not fare as well. Joe and Adrian had what seemed a good marriage. Good jobs, a beautiful home, two nice half-grown children, regular family vacations, all the amenities of an affluent lifestyle. But things went wrong somewhere. Adrian had always trusted her husband completely. One day it became known that, after 18 years of marriage, he was carrying on an affair with a co-worker. After some counseling and much soul-searching, Adrian decided to try to forgive and keep the marriage intact, if Joe would break up the affair. He promised, and it seemed as though things would be mended.

Then - and my heart bleeds for this poor woman - Adrian found out that Joe had carried on two other affairs in the past. The first affair occurred when she was pregnant with their first child. Joe lied at first, then admitted everything. He asked her forgiveness, but Adrian couldn't handle the present and the past all at one time. She suffered a nervous breakdown and asked for a divorce. The divorce is now final, and Adrian is on the mend. It will be slow, but she is a vibrant woman of 45, and she will soon have her life back together. Good luck and God Bless You, Adrian.

Another couple's story comes to mind. This one involves infidelity on the wife's part. Linda was a good wife and mother of two. Her handsome middle executive husband Ron was a good provider and did not want his wife to work. Linda had given up her teaching career when her daughter, now age nine, was born, and did not particularly care to return to work. This pleased Ron, and all seemed well in their world.

KEEP THE FLAME ALIVE

Linda had everything she wanted, except an attentive husband. How could he be attentive to his wife and family when he was "married" to his job? Ron was considered the absolute master of his house, not to be opposed in anything. He made all the major decisions, including where the family would vacation. Oh yes, he "donated" two weeks of his precious time to his family every year, to go on vacation.

Linda was very happy during the first few years, but then little "twinges" of dissatisfaction manifested themselves. Was taking kids to ballet lessons and little league games and scout meetings all there was to life? Add to that some long evenings after the children were in bed, waiting for MISTER BIG AND HANDSOME to come home from the office, just so she could have a few minutes with him before bedtime.

Ron, this good, hard working man, never thought that his wife may not be completely happy. He gave her "everything a girl could want." What else could he do?

Then it happened. A mutual friend - a man who could not compete with Ron in any way - began to pay attention to Linda. This young bachelor, Mike, lived with his mother, had few friends, and seemed to suffer from a mild form of depression on and off. Linda tells me she never thought of him as a lover prospect -- she never thought of anyone but her husband. But she felt sorry for this sad young man. (Yes, empathy or sympathy can lead to stronger feelings). So she invited him for a cup of coffee at the house when Ron was on a business tip. Harmless enough? Not really.

Boredom, loneliness, the lack of ego strokes (Linda couldn't even remember the last time Ron had told her she was pretty), and human weakness led to the catastrophe.

What happened could not be undone. The marriage ended in divorce. What a waste of such a beautiful family. And the tragedy was totally preventable.

Effects of Life Stages

One more couple almost lost their marriage, partially, because the wife was going through menopause and the *empty nest* syndrome all at the same time. Their beautiful twin daughters, to whom the mother had dedicated all the best years of her life, had gone off to college. This woman was hit by all the worst symptoms of menopause. She was not feeling well much of the time, and felt mildly depressed almost all of the time. On top of it all, she succumbed to eating binges and gained a lot of weight.

The result was not the friendship, ego strokes and empathy she was yearning to receive from her husband. Instead, she got disgusted looks, which she believed were directed at her expanding figure, and the inevitable question, "Are you going to go on a diet one of these days?" The well-known vicious cycle of overeating, depression and more overeating had this woman in its grips.

She began to fantasize about a physician friend of the family, a widower on whom she had a little "crush" for years. When she called him to tell him her many troubles, including that her husband did not even talk to her any more, she was ready for an affair with this sensitive man who had always been so nice to her.

But this health professional saw the complete picture. He sat down with her and explained that she was experiencing normal menopausal symptoms, but that some help may be needed to get over the worst years. Counseling was arranged. First the wife alone, then she and the physician persuaded her husband to accompany her. The marriage is intact now, and seems to be flourishing. On the advice of both the physician and the counselor, the woman has lost weight, is taking college courses and has learned to enjoy her post-menopausal years.

This is one story with a happy ending, because a friend did not take advantage of the situation. Instead, he advised this woman of the right course to take in order to find a solution to the problem.

The next chapter will have more on the stages of our lives.

In an article in the April 1995 Readers Digest titled "Can a Marriage Survive an Affair?" author Donna Brown Hogarty points out that affairs occur even in happy marriages. Sometimes they are the result of a personal crisis. According to this author, if the affair ends, the straying partner may have learned a lesson, and may be a better mate in the future.

In any case, don't use a past affair as a weapon in future marital fights. It will build more resentment for you by "reviving" your past pain, and for your partner, by making him or her realize that you have not forgiven.

Make Use of All the Help You Can Get

You will probably need help in working through your pain while the healing process is taking place. If you have faith in God, use it. Those who believe in God's help fare better in a crisis. Pastoral counseling can be very helpful. If you are not good at communicating, learn from a counselor, or from books.

Keep in mind that your partner needs healing too. If you want to save the marriage you must help your mate. Respect his or her feelings, even if you may think they are silly.

Now is the most critical time to keep the communication lines open. If there is a lack of communications, especially when it comes to failure to make needs known to each other, this can wreak further havoc with the marriage. If misunderstandings had caused estrangement in the past and perhaps brought on the affair, communicating is more important than ever. If communications are not vastly improved, the marriage may still be doomed, even after reconciliation. In other words, without communicating, there is not much hope for the ultimate survival of the relationship. So, keep talking, keep relating.

Make a pact that you can discuss the past without letting your tempers flare up. If you feel you need to talk about what happened, your partner must accept this. If you feel you must express your hurt and rage, do it by using "I" statements as explained in the communications chapter. Refrain from "dumping" accusations on your partner.

It will be helpful for the one who had the affair to discuss events leading up to it, and why it happened, but please do not rationalize too much. You need to muster the courage to admit a wrong done, then vow not to repeat it. In other words, draw valuable lessons from this, to prevent a recurrence. All partners must continually try not to place blame.

Honesty

Effective communication includes complete honesty. If a few little secrets were allowed before the affair, <u>none are allowed afterward</u>. Why? Because the betrayed partner is so highly sensitized that any little sign now points to a new affair in her or his mind. The other partner may also be sensitized, but in a different way. The betrayed partner may have done some "spying" to get to the bottom of things. This was probably a necessity at the time, and the wrongdoer should readily forgive this.

Likewise, he or she should not resent it if the *wounded* partner asks questions. Answering them honestly is essential. But after reconciliation and the promise that all the bad times are behind you, the spying must stop. The betrayed partner must try to trust, and in turn the other partner must work hard not to ever betray that trust again.

All this may take years. And there may be setbacks in the healing and forgiveness process. To repeat an important point, complete openness is essential. It can not be emphasized enough: <u>No more secrets!</u>

Time for Acceptance

In the above quoted article Donna Brown Hogarty states that people should not expect things to be the same after an affair, especially if the partners had been idealizing each other. After an affair, "You now must replace those ideas with a more sophisticated reality and accept each other's flaws and strengths." In other words, expecting things to be exactly as they were is unrealistic. Now is the time to try and see only the good in your mate. Here's why.

In order to justify his or her infidelity, your partner may have said unkind things about you, and the person he had the affair with may have "fanned the fire" in that respect, magnifying a negative image of the betrayed partner. Likewise, the betrayed partner probably built in his or her memory the worst image of the betrayer. Both partners need to erase these negative images from their memory.

If you continue to see the worst in the other, you will most likely get the worst. You need to get active and invoke in your mind the person you first fell in love with. Think of the reasons you fell in love with him or her, and search for those traits. They may be hard to find at first, but if you look, you will find them. Finding those good traits will help you learn to love your mate again.

In order to love another person, it is necessary that you love and take care of yourself first. Nourish your good traits. Practice being the person you want to be, to make it as easy as possible to revive your love for each other.

A Crack Doesn't Mean the Egg is Broken

An affair - real or *platonical* - does not have to end a relationship. Remember that sometimes a crisis is necessary to wake us up from our lethargy. For Jody and Jim, and many other couples I have talked to over the years, a revival, a new and better relationship was born out of the crisis. Give it a chance to work for you. Consider the alternative. In many cases it may be far better to salvage a relationship than to endure years of loneliness when you reach your twilight years.

CHAPTER VII

THE MENOPAUSE AND THE MALE MIDLIFE CRISIS

"And what do those life-stages have to do with my marriage?", you may say. Quite a bit.

These times in our lives are reflected by a decline in sex hormones. The hormonal changes are more marked in the female than in the male. The hormonal decrease leads to both physical and emotional changes, which, in turn, play a significant role in every aspect of our being.

These often troubled periods in our lives are natural passages, and they must be accepted by everyone. For some people, they exert minimal effects. For some, none of the effects are perceptible at all, yet for others these changes can be profound. In fact, they may bring on so much emotional turmoil that they can *make or break* a relationship.

The best you can do in preparation for these passages in life is to get strong before arriving there. If a marriage is not built on a good foundation - if intimacy, communication, trust, and love have diminished or vanished over the years - the union can topple, or at least be severely shaken. In fact, in some cases repair may not be possible.

In his book *His Needs, Her Needs: How Affair-proof Is Your Marriage?*, Willard F. Harley, Jr. compares relationships with bank accounts. According to this splendid analogy, deposits in the relationship bank account can be anything from a little extra kindness to a great gesture of love. Withdrawals can be little annoyances or big, unresolved fights. "Deposits" and "withdrawals" are made on a daily basis. The greater the balance in the account, the healthier the relationship, hence the better its tolerance to troubles. Thus, a happy marriage is backed by good reserves, whereas unhappy partners have no resources left in their relationship accounts.

So, if your balance is in the black because you have worked at your marriage, have done more kind things for each other than unkind ones, some withdrawals during hard times will not put the account in the red. But if the account balance has been around zero, even a small withdrawal can put it in the red.

It would be wise to check your relationship account balance before the tough years come. If the account is *in good shape*, you can face these times without falling apart. These hard times, as well as other stressful periods such as illness, should be faced by a couple together. Not, as so often occurs, separately and with feelings of resentment against each other.

Let's explore what people can do for themselves and their partners when times of physical and emotional troubles come.

The Menopause

Menopause is the time in a woman's life when the ovaries stop producing ova (eggs), and the production of the hormones that control menstruation ceases.

Hot flashes, dizziness, night sweats, headaches, insomnia, bouts with depression, and sometimes urge or stress incontinence, are some of the classic menopausal symptoms. The latter is manifested as a weakness of the bladder's upper sphincter muscle, resulting in leakage of a drop of urine when the urge to urinate is not immediately relieved. It is not complete incontinence, but nevertheless frustrating and sometimes embarrassing.

Not every woman experiences all of these, and some may experience none. However, a great majority of women come to know at least some of them well.

Regardless of what specific symptoms a woman has, even if she does not experience any of the above, her body must adjust to changes that may have an impact on her sex life, her psyche, her looks. Among these symptoms, a decline in vaginal wetness during sexual arousal, and decreased vaginal elasticity, can lead to a loss of interest in sex.

With the availability of HRT (hormone replacement therapy), menopausal symptoms can be remedied. But since the ovaries begin slowly shutting down their estrogen (female hormone) production long before the actual onset of menopause - typically in a woman's early forties - the symptoms of menopause can *sneak up* on a woman when she doesn't even realize what's happening.

She may be ashamed of her symptoms and act out in other ways, often in the form of sudden crying spells for no apparent reason. These reactions, of course, only worsen her mental and physical condition. Her vaginal dryness may be misinterpreted by her husband. He may worry that he can no longer excite her, or worse, that she no longer loves him. All of this can have profound adverse effects on a man.

Add to this the realization that menopause signals the end of her child-bearing years (although she could still get pregnant for some time), the loss of her youthful appearance, and the fear of the dreaded bone thinning (osteoporosis), and a woman's mood may worsen.

Furthermore, many women suffer through the "empty nest" syndrome at the same time as the arrival of the menopause. Some women have prepared themselves for the departure of their children and do well at *letting go*, others grieve intensely, as though they had lost the child forever.

A woman may turn to stress-eating at that time. She knows she is destroying her health by gaining weight, she knows that her husband is looking unfavorably at her rounding figure, but she can't stop!

During this stressful time, a woman may be perceived as a veritable *pain in the derriere* by her husband, who repeatedly tries to find out what's wrong. He may attempt to console her, without success.

Can you see a vicious cycle beginning here? If a couple's communication is not good at this time, if marital intimacy and love are not *up to par*, in other words, if their *relationship bank account* is not in the black, an erosion of the marriage will be the inevitable result.

His Side of the Story

As mentioned above, the sexual and emotional changes occurring in a menopausal woman may exert an adverse effect on her husband as well. He may feel angry and rejected because his wife does not want to be touched, complaining of vaginal dryness and vaginal spasms (vaginismus). As a consequence of his wife's troubles, he may no longer be able to have or to maintain an erection. Can you see a vicious cycle in full swing?

What Can Be Done?

Needless to dwell further on what all of this can do to a marriage. So let's concentrate on what you can do if this affects you.

First and foremost: COMMUNICATE! Marital partners must be open about everything they feel, mentally and physically. Your partner needs to know what hurts, and what feels good. So speak up instead of *moping around*.

Put yourself in your mate's shoes. Be understanding and patient. You are partners. You are in this together. The Bible says: "When two people are joined together in marriage, they become one flesh" (Gen. 2:24).

So stick together, work it out. And remember, help is available. See your doctor to discuss hormone replacement therapy to relieve the physical symptoms and prevent osteoporosis. If you are postmenopausal and have not had hormone replacement therapy, you may ask your physician about a bone density test to determine the status of your bones. If the test shows that you have osteoporosis, several drugs are available to treat the condition. Among them, "Fosamax", appears to be the most promising.

If you need help in the "communications department" of your marriage, don't delay in finding a professional or pastoral counselor. These professionals have the training and experience to help you, step by step, to establish an effective communications system in your marriage. Taking this step could mean the renewal and revival of your relationship.

Do remember, the troubled times will pass. Instead of succumbing to your downcast state of mind, perhaps thinking about old age coming soon, tell yourself that you are "just getting started" ... at whatever you are going to do for many years to come.

During the middle years, most women are free to *follow their star*. They can now do the things they never had time to do before, and this can be a wonderful time of renewal in a woman's life.

So it's time to stop feeling sorry for yourself. Get your physical problems repaired and then forget about the menopause. Because, the more you dwell on it the more power it will gain over you. Don't let it. Find meaningful and enjoyable activities. *Re-invent* yourself. Reach for the stars. They may be closer than you think.

The Male Midlife Crisis

Much more is known about menopause than the male midlife crisis. Since so much is known about the menopause, and successful treatment by a physician is just a phone call away, I will not dwell further on this passage in a woman's life.

Since the male midlife crisis is a more "hushed-up" subject, and less is written about it than the menopause, I will devote more explanation to that portion of this chapter.

Your husband may fly off the handle about every little thing, blaming you or the kids for every small nuisance that he encounters. He may, for the first time in your marriage, look at other women. He may be quiet and *grumpy*, and when you ask, "What's wrong?", he may snap: "Nothing." He may drink more than he used to. He may stay at work longer than ever before, and find all sorts of "male only" functions and meetings to go to.

Your husband may have little interest in sex, at least not with you. He may even think of buying - for himself only - a classy sports car.

The sports car brings to mind a joke I once heard. To paraphrase: Two women are standing in a driveway, talking. When a red sporty car drives up, one of the women says: "There comes my husband in his brand new *midlife Chrysler...*"

But the real thing is not funny at all. If you have become the brunt of your husband's *grumpy* moods, but he shuts you out when you try to please him and help him, life can be miserable.

And that is just what he may do. He may get angry when you try to communicate. When you decide to give him his *space*, he doesn't like that, either. *Why has he changed? What have I done wrong?*, you think.

Your friends may tell you, "He's going through the midlife crisis. Just wait it out. He'll return to normal after a while." Easier said than done. You know your husband is agonizing over something, he seems miserable and he's making you miserable, and he doesn't seem to know what he really wants.

In his mind your husband may keep blaming you. *Doesn't she realize I'm under a lot of pressure at work? Doesn't she realize that it isn't easy for a man to have sex when he is dead tired? At least that secretary at the office seems like she would understand if I talked to her. But I shouldn't be thinking of other women. I'm a happily married man. Am I?*

He continues to feel somehow trapped and wanting to be free. Free of his job, his wife, his kids, even his parents and his friends. At times he just wants to run away, never to be seen or heard from again.

This brings to mind a recent occurrence I have shed tears over. It involves Frank, a family man in his late fifties, who recently took early retirement from his job in order to pursue his hobby of training and racing sled dogs. When I saw Frank at a dog sled race several weeks after his retirement, he seemed *overjoyed*. He said that now he could finally do what he loves more than any other activity in the world. He could finally *live his dream* of spending endless hours on the trail with his dogs, not only on weekends.

A few weeks later I talked to Frank's wife Norma. What she told me made my whole body go *numb*. After the time I saw Frank with a big smile on his face, things had suddenly gone *downhill* for him, and hence their marriage. Norma said, without warning, he stopped eating, lost weight, sat around brooding, and would not talk to her at all. In fact, he seemed to have lost interest in his sled team, the very reason he took early retirement.

Then one day he loaded the team, several sleds, equipment and dog food in the truck and took off to a northern state as he had done on many winter weekends over the last two decades. In fact, Norma had gone with him on many of those trips in the past. She spent endless hours, patiently sitting in the truck while he trained his team. Norma did not enjoy those trips, but went along because she loved her husband. When he left this last time, she thought he'd come back refreshed and over his little *funk* in a few days.

Frank did come back, but with an empty truck. Asked what happened, he said, "I sold my team," and then announced to his shocked wife that he was leaving her. He was very "nasty", in Norma's words, packed some of his belongings and left.

What the wife found out after Frank left was this. He moved in with another woman (Norma had never suspected an affair). To magnify the tragedy, his dogs turned up in several states along the highways, where most of them were picked up by the state police. Two were never found. One of the two was a 12-year-old dog. Said Norma: "If Frank had pampered that dog for the rest of his days, he could not have paid back the loyalty this faithful companion had given him during all those years on the trails of the north country".

Through many phone calls, Norma found out that Frank had given several of the dogs away (not sold), and had also given away all of the equipment and the dog food. Frank started the journey home with eight of his faithful companions, without dog food. Had he planned to shoot the remaining dogs when he got home, and then changed his mind and turned them loose? No one may ever know but Frank.

Besides committing cruelty to animals, this man also threw away many thousands of dollars, because, it was a superbly trained, *top notch* racing team he "*disposed of.*"

What "snapped" in this man who, during the two decades I knew him, always appeared like the "rock of Gibraltar?" Was it a late - unusually severe - midlife crisis? Or was it a complete (temporary) loss of sanity? And what will happen next? Has Frank since gone for help to resolve this unusually severe crisis? Or will it resolve with the passage of time? I sincerely hope so. For the time, I only have questions in this case. No answers. But there is a bright spot in this tragic story. Norma is resilient. She is making fast progress in rebuilding her life, and she is doing well. This brave woman focuses only on the future, on looking ahead and not back.

The midlife crisis usually hits a man anywhere between the ages of 35 and 50. It can last from several months to several years. But, just as with the menopause, some men hardly notice they are going through this stage. These lucky guys may not experience any of these symptoms, while others may be hard hit.

Although the menopause is sometimes referred to as a type of midlife crisis, the male midlife crisis is different from the menopause. Men do not have radical hormonal decreases, as do women. The male hormonal decline is very gradual. It is so slight that it does not seem to affect a man's sexual functioning until the senior years, although other physiological manifestations such as overweight, hypertension (high blood pressure) or prostate problems can have adverse effects on a man's sexual performance.

Thus, there are no marked physical reasons for the male midlife crisis. The crisis I am describing is an emotional one, manifested by mood swings, irritability, depression, and loss of his sense of wellbeing. Yet a man will emphatically deny having it. He may wonder if others are experiencing similar symptoms, but he won't talk about it to his wife or other men.

After all, a man has been programmed from childhood to repress his emotions, and somewhere during midlife all the stress built up over many years *catches up*. Now emotions suppressed for decades begin to surface, not as clear thoughts, but all mixed up. He may be afraid of emotions he can't even interpret. And he's not supposed to be afraid, either.

All he was ever taught about emotions was to suppress them. And now they bother him, making him miserable.

But why can't he talk to his wife? He probably wouldn't know how to start. Most likely he doesn't know what real intimacy means. In his marriage, sex has probably been the closest he ever came to experiencing intimacy. He just wouldn't know how to respond to his wife's requests or demands for intimacy, except to push her further away from him. He may even become sexually dysfunctional, a most dreaded occurrence for any man.

But why don't these feelings go away?, he may think. Because he is going through a normal developmental phase, and it takes time.

At midlife, a man begins to realize the high price he has been paying for never showing emotions, never revealing his true personality, in fact he may not even know what his true personality is. He has played the game he was taught, namely, to hide his emotions, to the point where his wife believes he doesn't have any. But this is not so. He may not know himself, but deep inside he knows that he too needs both physical and verbal affection - to give and to receive it. But it is so hard to re-connect with his wife if the two have already drifted apart.

This is why men in this stage are so vulnerable to affairs. Not that affairs are planned. They usually "just happen". The man may find some relief from his depressed state, a lift, so to speak, by getting involved in an extramarital affair. Or, the affair may just be a *platonical* relationship which can be just as damaging to his marriage.

The tragedy is that usually divorce follows. And, as already mentioned, a man rarely marries the woman who triggered the breakup of his marriage. Left behind is a broken home and a lonely man who wishes he had his family back.

People should know that the midlife crisis is part of the normal growing process. In her book *Passages*, Gail Sheehy documented the middle years for both males and females. She emphasized that if this stage is not successfully dealt with, it will continue to haunt you from time to time.

Midlife is a time a man can free himself from the constraints of his childhood, the unreasonable expectations he has been trying to live up to. These are, as already mentioned, to always be strong, never vulnerable, and never show feelings. Now is the time to shake those antiquated, stress and disease producing beliefs, and become more human, more accepting of himself and others, and last but not least, more open about his emotions, closer to the partner he chose for life when he said "I Do!" This partner has probably spent the last several decades wondering why her big strong prince doesn't ever express his emotions, the sort of thing she never had any trouble exhibiting. She never realized that he may have the same emotions she has, the same desire to be himself, to share himself, but that his resolve to live up to his previous conditioning has always been stronger than any desire to be himself.

What Men Can Do

Instead of drifting apart, here is a chance to regain some of the marital intimacy lost over the years, to re-connect with your soulmate. Most wives would love to have the chance to help their husbands to overcome their anguish, to decrease the feelings of isolation they may have. The fact that male suicides increase with age seems to indicate that the midlife transition is not always successfully dealt with.

I would say this to any man going through the anguish of the middle years, the confused emotions, the depression, the self-evaluation, the thought: *What have I done with my life?* You will need to do a lot of soul-searching to get to know and understand yourself first, try to *come to grips* with the emotions that churn inside of you, your needs, your fears. Then take the emotional risk involved in intimacy, try to get closer to your wife, share your thoughts with her. Give her a chance to accept you and love you as you are, as a human being, not *superman*. Had Frank given Norma a chance to understand him, they may still be together today, and Frank's loyal dog companions would not have been *sacrificed*.

If you show some confidence in your partner for life, this will be a *load off her mind* too. In fact, your wife will very likely turn out to be the best friend you ever had. After all, who knows more about you than anyone else, and is still with you?

If you would rather talk to a neutral party first, get professional or pastoral counseling. These people have the training and experience to understand your problems. If you do talk to a professional, try not to shut your wife out completely. Face it together. Just as you may have been frustrated about her menopausal behavior patterns, she feels frustrated and helpless about yours. Each needs to muster a lot of patience, for as long as these hard times continue.

Wives need to realize that changes do not occur overnight. You have to give your partner as much space as he needs. Do know that your partner's midlife problems are **not**

your fault. You did not make your partner feel the way he does. Our feelings and actions are still our own responsibility, and the sooner each gets out of the blaming and condemning mode, the better. If your husband needs more time to work out his emotions, you will have to give it to him. If you want to spend more time together but he wants to run off and play golf, don't get pushy. If you demand he spend the time with you, he may try harder to get away. It's not you he wants to get away from, but the feelings he has been suppressing for so long. So give him space. He'll come around faster.

And don't put your own life on hold. Make your own plans. Do things that make you feel good. You've earned it during all those years of nurturing the family. Be as relaxed and attractive as you can. If you've been an "open book" about everything that's inside of you, perhaps you could try to become a little mysterious. Most men like that. Remember that he is having his struggle and just can not reach out to you yet. But he will.

Maybe you are all through menopause, and maybe you can remember a time when you threw yourself on the bed, crying for no reason, and not letting him near you to comfort you? Remember the mental anguish you experienced? Remember the patience he had? Your anguish was probably briefer than his, but that's because you are different. A man just has to suffer longer because of his upbringing and the emotional *hangups* created in him.

Partners

There's no getting around it. The partners have to allow each other the time that is needed to resolve their emotional dilemmas. But as soon as you can, re-connect, so that you can have a close relationship again. Approve of each other. Pay compliments, look for the good traits, and ignore the others. An ancient Hindu proverb says: "An unwelcome visitor will soon leave." Translated to unwelcome traits, there is a better chance they'll disappear if you ignore them.

Someone has to start. If you start complimenting your partner, you will create in him or her a tendency to pay back the compliment, to give you approval. Form that *mutual admiration society*, where the atmosphere is safe for both of you to reveal your feelings and dreams. The rewards are great.

The middle years can be a great new beginning. Enjoy them, together. Get strong now, individually and in your partnership. The frailties of old age will be upon you some day. As previously mentioned, these will be much harder to face if your communication lines are not open, if your relationship is not what it should be, a union built on love, commitment, trust and understanding. The choice is yours. The time is now. Don't throw the opportunity away.

Summary of Both Crises

In many ways, the emotional conflicts of the middle years are similar for men and women. So, if you have arrived at this passage and you feel an emptiness and dissatisfaction with everything that was dear and important to you during your younger years, you are not alone. If you struggle with questions regarding what could give your life more meaning, value, and fulfillment, the age-old question of immortality we all struggle with may be *knocking at your door* at this time of your life.

Becoming more spiritual - and by spiritual I do not necessarily mean religious - may help. Turning to God in prayer holds much promise for many people. It may still be on an unconscious level for you, but midlife is the time when people begin to be concerned with their immortal souls. People who seek a close communion with God during their middle years are able to face the senior years with more joy and less depression than do nonbelievers.

At such times one may fall back on the book, *In The Middle of This Road We Call Our Life*, by James W. Jones. According to this author, our lives acquire meaning if we are connected to something beyond our own ego. Jones tells us that the midlife crisis is not a sign that one is suddenly becoming insane, but rather, a symbol of maturity. He advises us to look for the deeper meaning behind our unrest and discontent, to move past it, to accept it as part of our growth, the next step in our human development.

Final Sum-Up

All passages of life - from childhood to teens to young adulthood to the thirties and the forties, and on - have their unique problems. And the middle years are no exception. We have gained much wisdom and life experience during all of those years. Now we need to use this wisdom to get over just one more hurdle.

Clearing that hurdle successfully will make us more human, and grant us clear sailing into the next decades. We all have the choice to *use it or lose it*. What I mean is, make the effort. Deal with your emotions, seek professional help if necessary. Also, take care of your body with good nutrition and a healthy level of exercise.

KEEP THE FLAME ALIVE

Seek help for any physical problems you may have. Strengthen your marital ties. *Put it all together* for a brilliant, wise, happy, healthy *finished product*. Remember, this stage too will pass. Consider it a learning experience for a better tomorrow, for you and your soulmate.

CHAPTER VIII

HOW OUR EMOTIONS AFFECT OUR HEALTH

Stress, the most popular *buzzword* of recent times, is on everyone's mind nowadays. And rightly so, because it affects our most precious possession, our health.

To briefly define stress, it is what we feel when the demands on us exceed our coping abilities. The origin of stress may be of an internal nature, for example, illness. Or, the stress may be due to external forces beyond our control, for instance, loss of a loved one, a wrong done to us. Loss may not necessarily be death, but it could be separation from a person, or simply loss of the love and affection of someone we cherish.

How we deal with the stress brought on by such situations depends on our response to them, as well as our emotional hardiness. Since illness is often brought on by emotional stress, I will explain some of the mechanisms that play a role in this development, especially as related to the loss of, or betrayal by a loved one. I will also mention some preventive or coping skills needed to deal with the situation without losing our health.

The Mind-Body Connection

In her book, *You Can Heal Your Life,* author Louise L. Hay talks about junky food creating a toxic body, and that negative, destructive thinking patterns eventually lead to a toxic mind. I wholeheartedly agree with this author's concept. It follows, that destructive thinking not only produces a toxic mind, but a toxic body as well.

It is well known that people who can not or will not vent their emotions or their anger feel they have no control over their own lives. They feel powerless and hopeless. Patients with cancer are often those who have suppressed anger all their lives. Thus, the fact that considerably more men die of cancer than women comes as no surprise, given that most men do not show emotions. Feeling hopeless and depressed exerts adverse effects on the immune system, and cancer is a consequence of a breakdown of the immune system.

Louise Hay confirms this in her book. She recounts how her stored-up anger resulting from a childhood of sexual abuse had culminated in what she calls the disease of resentment, cancer. She credits learning to let go of her painful past and the low self esteem it had created in her, learning to forgive those who had hurt her, and to love herself, with her cure of the cancer. Ms. Hay claims to have cured herself by means of alternative treatments and mind-healing.

Consequences of Anger and Stress

Working with chronic pain patients in the past (many of whom had cancer), I was able to observe some of the patterns of anger and resentment. These destructive emotions often dated back to childhood. Feelings of guilt (*I don't deserve to get better*), blaming, low self esteem, and other self destructive patterns of the mind dominated these unfortunate individuals.

Likewise, as a co-leader of stress reduction support groups I can see the patterns clearly, the patterns of prolonged, unresolved stress leading to illness. Only

when people learn to deal with their stresses, when they learn to cope with the inevitable ones and reduce those over which
they have control, can their physical problems be resolved. In other words, the psychological and physical components - the mind
and the body - have to do the work together.
And since the mind is in control, or at
least should be, the mind should be put to
work first.

So where is the connection? Thoughts
lead to feelings, and feelings influence
hormones. Some of the hormones involved are
neurotransmitters (brain chemicals). A neu-
rotransmitter is the substance that acts in
the brain and nervous system to bring about
changes in the body, both positive ones and
negative ones. For instance, when you stimulate neurotransmitters called endorphins by
exercising or other rewarding activities,
your mood brightens. The calm, serene state
of mind, in turn, leads to a reduction of
other chemicals that speed the body up,
especially adrenalin (also called epineph-
rine).

Stress stimulates the production of
adrenalin which is secreted by the adrenal
glands, as well as the adrenal hormone cortisone. These substances are necessary for
normal body functioning, but they are produced in excess when stimulated by stress.

The Fight or Flight Response

Stress manifests as an arousal response
in the body, also called the fight or flight
response. The fight or flight response goes
back to ancient times, when our primitive
ancestors needed high levels of adrenal hormones for survival.

These substances, especially adrenalin, produced rapidly and in larger than the normal amounts, gave these people the extra strength and speed to survive by either running from, or fighting with an enemy. It works like this: Large amounts of adrenalin raise the blood pressure and speed up the heart rate. High levels of cortisone contribute to a rise in blood glucose (sugar), to supply the muscles with the energy needed for physical defense or running from an enemy. This is precisely what the sedentary folks of modern times do not need.

Modern man usually does not have the need for the changes brought on by the excessive production of these hormones. Because we usually will not fight physically, nor will we flee if we are confronted with a challenging situation. Thus, the body functions designed for coping with such a situation are *revved up* for nothing. This takes its toll in the form of wear and tear on the body, eventually leading to illness.

For example, someone upset or hurt you, and the anger that welled up in you caused an increase of the stress hormones, so you would have the energy and muscle strength to *beat the heck* out of this person. Since you are a dignified individual, you don't resort to this method, so your adrenalin is wildly coursing around your body in your bloodstream, and your blood sugar and blood pressure are too high, and your heart beats at its maximum, and there is no place for the adrenalin and sugar to go, and your heart is wearing itself out for nothing. All of this raises the tension, hence stress, in your body to unhealthy levels.

Not all stress is detrimental, and not all stress is perceived equally by everyone. The greatest contributor to the development of really damaging stress is frustration, especially when it is of a chronic nature. You have nowhere to run, no outlet for the excess of adrenal hormones. This buildup of tension can eventually lead to illnesses such as heart disease, depression, ulcers, even cancer.

Survival Tactics

Commitment to one's work and family, the feeling of being in control of one's life, the ability to cope with change, and seeing difficult situations as challenges rather than threats, are key points.

Emotional stresses can build up over years, especially in a marriage where conflicts are never resolved. These stresses gain control over the individual. Thus, we have to wage war against loss of control over our own lives, if we want to survive and be happy and healthy. We need to work on stress perception, to see certain stresses as challenges and not uncontrollable forces and threats. We need to work on stress reduction, by recognizing those stressful situations which can be changed, change them, and by recognizing what can not be changed, and learn to live with it.

For example, my friend Laura's husband, Harry, was late for dinner almost all the time, and this caused her many tears of frustration hence stress. Not that he didn't try, but having to close the doors of his small insurance agency himself every night, there was always that last phone call that made him 10, 15 or sometimes 30 minutes late. Laura finally decided to discuss a change of dinner time. Both partners agreed that dinner should be 30 minutes later than it had been. Then, if Harry happened to be home early, he had to wait for dinner. So in Laura's case, she solved her own problem of

constant frustration by changing dinner
time. Result: Laura prevented stress by
changing a situation she could change.

Perhaps you have a similar situation.
For example, your partner is habitually
late, but for no special reason. In that
case you may just have to eat by yourself
some of the time, and heat your mate's dinner up later. This may not be ideal, but it
could save you the frustration of waiting
for your own dinner. Since you can not
change another person's behavior unless that
person wants to change, your adjustment to
the situation would reduce your stress.

Nick grew up in a household where
everything was put in its proper place. His
mother was a meticulous homemaker. He only
assumed that Cindy, his new bride, would be
like mother. But Cindy did not share Nick's
neatness. She was a messy housekeeper, and
having lived alone for 10 years before she
married Nick, she wasn't about to change her
ways. Nick picked up after her constantly,
and his frustration grew.

Many arguments about her clutter -
books, magazines, shoes, lingerie - took
place. During these fights she called him a
cleanfreak who was *obsessed* with neatness,
and he called her a lazy slob. Lots of bitterness built up between them. But Nick
loved his wife too much to give up on their
marriage because of her messiness, so he
finally *confessed* his problem to his mother.
She liked her daughter-in-law. So the last
thing she wanted for the couple was a divorce. Nick's mother suggested that her son
talk to a counselor, alone.

The counselor made Nick realize that he
may never be able to change someone who had
grown up in a messy household such as the
one Cindy grew up in. In fact, Cindy would

probably not change any more than he, having grown up in a neat household, would change.

The counselor taught Nick coping techniques. He made him realize that he should relax because he could not change the situation, to *let go and let God*. The counselor also suggested that Nick relax his own standards of neatness just a little. Yes, Cindy got away with it ... the messiness. But what is more important, how the house looks or the preservation of the marriage?

You may say, "If she had really loved Nick she would have changed," and yes, that thought crossed my mind too. But who are we to judge? Cindy's background made it hard for her, and I hope that her love for her husband will eventually meet him halfway. For the time, relaxing and not *forcing* a change is helping Nick cope with stress. And this will hopefully extend his lifespan.

We all need to work on our emotional hardiness, our *survival*.

So what does it really take to be a *survivor* of the relentless pressures and heartaches that plague us, especially in our relationships?

- We need to work on not allowing our hearts to be broken.
- We need to work on not letting external forces, situations, or people control us, hence build stresses within us.
- We need to let go of the things we can not change, as Nick did.
- We need to get so hardy - I like to call it tough - that no one can hurt us even if they try.

Feeling in Control Makes Big Difference

In the perception of stress, feeling in control of our lives versus the feeling of having no control makes the difference. If

you feel someone, especially the person you
love, or something, especially that loved
one's actions, occupy your mind excessively,
to the point where these emotions have control over you, the stress can be damaging to
your health. Add to that uncertainty and in-
security about your relationship, and the
frustration and worry intensify. Eventually,
all of this will lead to a weakening or complete breakdown of your immune system hence
illness.

So, if you are unhappy about the
actions of your wife or husband, you need to
make the effort not to let these factors
control how you feel. Begin by communicating
your feelings. Let your mate know that his
or her actions disturb you. Seek counseling
if needed. If this gets no result, you will
have to let go of the situation.

As Cindy's husband Nick came to realize
with the help of the counselor, the only
person we can ever change is ourselves. So,
to reduce stress, you need to work on being
the person you want to be, and attend to
your own agenda. Play on the only instrument
you have: YOU.

It is said that what counts is not what
happens to us, but what happens in us. We
need to let go. Thoughts and perceptions
produce emotions. And we can all control our
thoughts or how we perceive a situation. We
can "awfulize" everything, or we can say
"it's not all that bad".

If you take some of these steps - take
your mind off the changes you want to see in
your partner and attend to your own person
- your battle against stress and illness has
just taken a turn towards eventual victory.
That's easier said than done. I agree, and,
speaking from experience, I didn't say it
was easy. But tell me, isn't it worth a try?

You owe it to yourself, your health, in fact, the entire health care system of this country.

Case Histories

My friend Jennifer takes the Christian approach. When she found out her husband of 18 years was having an affair, her first reaction was - you guessed it - the collapse of her whole world. But not for long. This woman lives her life by the Holy Bible - and her response was this: "I know that God will answer my prayers, that my husband will return to me." Jennifer believes that it is a wife's job to love her husband in good times and bad, *'til death do us part'*, and that it is God's job to change him. She achieved her heart's desire, but it took a long time. How long? Actually, several years.

This woman found her strength in God, and she remained healthy throughout her long ordeal of fighting - and waiting - to get her husband back. Persistence, patience, and the *let go and let God* approach to her problem *saw her through* the worst years of her life.

My friend Ann went through similar heartbreak, but she eventually gave up. One day in 1995 she found out that John, her husband of 21 years, had an affair with another woman. Ann had stood by John through years of recurring bouts with depression, during which he drank heavily and was suicidal at times. He treated her and their teen-age daughter in an unloving, rude manner during those episodes.

John told both his wife and daughter that he did not love them and wanted no part of his family. Under psychiatric care, he always *came around*. During his "remissions" John was polite but not loving, and Ann knew something was wrong with their marriage. He lost all interest in sex and told his wife that the antidepressant medication made him impotent. He did not let his wife get close to him, and refused to relate. He ignored his daughter.

Times were rough, but Ann did not give up. She told me she loved John so much, that she would stay with him despite the way he treated her and their daughter, and that she felt she could never live without him, no matter what he did.

Ann's commitment to her marriage vows was admirable, but this made her vulnerable to great pain. She had made her husband the center of her world, and she wanted nothing to do with change. Her's was a perfect case of total dependency on another human being. Even though John was not directly trying to control his wife, indirectly he did. He controlled her life because she had tied it so closely to his that - with the exception of her daughter - nothing else mattered.

Another bout with depression had ended. Things once again seemed to go along smoothly, though without closeness between husband and wife or father and daughter. The two had learned to accept this, and it strengthened the mother-daughter bond.

Then came the catastrophe. One day John said, "I'm leaving." The shock hit like a ton of bricks. He told Ann that he loved another woman, and admitted that the affair had gone on for three months. I need not describe how devastated Ann was. She later found out that affairs had been a steady pattern during all those years when she attended to her *poor sick man*, taking him to doctors and psychiatrists, and suffering through the verbal abuses and threats of suicide. Ann never found out whether the depression came first, or the affairs.

Ann felt helpless, hopeless, sick. She just wanted to end her own life. She said that, after John had left, she sat on the stairs crying endlessly, maybe an hour, maybe more (Linda, her daughter, was at school). Then, a sudden surge of energy and determination came over her. Ann got on her feet, washed her face and began to put her thoughts in order.

Ann related to me that she said to herself, aloud: "Enough is enough. I'm free of you now. This is the end of my marriage, but it is not the end of me. I'm not finished. I will show the world how much spunk I have left in this 45-year-old body. I have my beautiful daughter to take care of, plus myself. I will get my life back together. No one is going to stop me." Ann said she thought to herself, *Sure I still love him, but he has treated us so badly the last few years, it's not worth trying to keep him any more. Besides, he was the worst lover I ever had, so who needs him anyway* ... She said the last thought suddenly made her roar with laughter. I believe God sent her the laughing spell to help her relax a little, hence alleviating stress.

During those tough years of John's depression episodes, knowing how dependent Ann was on John, I worried about what would happen if John ever left her or if things got so bad that she would have to leave, but I should not have worried. Ann pulled herself together immediately after her husband left.

The divorce was a long, drawn-out affair due to problems with the property settlement, but it is now final. Ann has been attending a post-divorce support group. She has made many new friends, revived her interest in arts and crafts, and has a part time job. Ann is proud of Linda, who is an honor student and track star. Now, more than a year after the divorce, mother and daughter are closer than ever, and they have weathered the storm. They have passed the test with flying colors. Although initially plagued by insomnia and frequent headaches, Ann remained healthy.

The reason Ann remained healthy following the betrayal by the person to whom she had given many of the best years of her life is obvious: Ann took control over her life back into her own hands before it was too late. By not letting her stresses become chronic, she helped her immune system not to succumb to illness.

More Coping Methods

Support groups can help as far as stress reduction goes. Many other methods have proven useful as well. Here are some.

- Take a walk or jog or swim, or do some other exercise, and you will feel their mood-boosting and stress-reducing power. Regular exercisers tend to handle stress better than sedentary persons.

- Making an effort to relax is high on the list of stress/tension reducers. It lowers the heart rate and blood pressure, while reducing muscle tension. Taking deep, slow breaths, expanding your lungs all the way down to your diaphragm (the so-called belly breathing), concentrating only on your breathing or visualizing a favorite, calm scene, listening to calming music, prayer, meditation, yoga... The possibilities are almost endless.

Exercising to exhaustion has always proven the best stress reduction method for me, but I do not propose that anyone who is not in top physical condition do this. It is far safer, and perhaps even more effective, to stick with the other methods. In order to manage your stresses, you must find the right level of activity. One that will stimulate you enough to keep your spirits up and your body systems functioning, without causing an overload.

There is help available for those who need some guidance in the art of stress reduction, for instance, relaxation tapes, books, biofeedback and even hypnosis. Health professionals and counselors can be of great help in any stress reduction program.

As mentioned in an earlier chapter, laughter, even at yourself, especially in the company of good friends, is one of the best stress reducers. Laughing at yourself does require a good self concept. This will shield you against embarrassment.

As I already described, I have my own method to stimulate laughter, in the form of a list of funny things that happened to me in the past, some dating back to childhood. If I need a good laugh and I can't find anything to laugh about, I can always pull out my little joy list. *That will do it every time!*

You can start your own joy list. Just sit down and think of funny things from the past, even if they were embarrassing and not funny when they happened. Now they probably are, if you want them to be. Remember that humor works better in stressful situations than anger.

Studies have shown that touching lowers the blood pressure and increases the amount of stress-reducing neurotransmitters (brain chemicals). So, couples, hold hands whenever you can. YOU WILL FEEL THE BENEFITS.

Charitable work is another stress reducer and health builder. We can do a lot for ourselves by doing things for others. During unhappy times, it can help to see other people who may have a worse burden to carry. Giving to others can spell good health for the giver.

There is one small danger involved in this. Sometimes people plunge so deeply into subliminal activities that they numb themselves to their own problems, failing to deal with them.

Erika, a good friend of mine, is trying to *numb* the pain of her loveless marriage by totally devoting herself to an immigrant family she has only known for a short time. These people are very grateful for all she does for them, showering her with affection. This is what's missing in her marriage, and to Erika, "It is so wonderful to be wanted and appreciated again."

Thus a *co-dependency* developed. "They need me, and I need them." But sooner or later Erika must realize that being part of this family is not a normal situation, nor can it be permanent. Someday the intensity of this new friendship will diminish or end, and then Erika must deal with her own problems again.

So remember, if you are a great giver - which is certainly synonymous with a wonderful person - don't forget about yourself completely. Don't ignore your relationship with your mate or other family members and friends. Give some attention to yourself. Make sure your own needs do not go unfulfilled. Don't be a *martyr*. FIND THE RIGHT BALANCE!

A social support group of good friends has been proven to be both a stress reducer and longevity builder. Becoming an active member of a church can enhance one's social network, reduce stresses and decrease the risk of illness. I believe that belonging to an accepting and caring community, while simultaneously nourishing your spiritual side, is one of the best time investments you can make in coping with stress.

Studies on select groups of Mormon males found a 50 percent reduction of cancer risk and a 35 percent reduction of heart attack risk as compared to non-Mormon men. Investigations of other religious groups have produced similar results. Adventists have been found to use tranquilizers less frequently than non-Adventists. Mental illness, anxiety and tension, and troubles with interpersonal relationships have been shown to be less frequent occurrences in this group as well.

Of all Christian churches, the Born Again Christians are among the most positive and most cheerful. They do not accept illness as a fact of life, and thus seem to have less illness. This group shows the world that, when you live a God centered life and abide by the 10 commandments, everything in life works better, including, and especially, relationships. This spells peace of mind, a great stress reducer. There simply is no room for gloom and negative emotions in the philosophy of a Born Again Christian.

Another very positive group is called Silent Unity, School of Christianity. Adherents to Unity principles believe that, with God's help, we create our own peace and harmony. One of their principles is: *Let Go, Let God.* In other words, let go of worry and strife, and let God take care of the situation.

This doesn't mean that people subscribing to this *don't worry be happy* philosophy are *Pollyannas*. They work hard on the things they can change, mainly themselves, and leave things they can not change to God. We are reminded that the Bible refers to the *sin of worry.*

Members of the above described groups believe in the power of prayer and meditation as great enhancers of peace of mind, hence stress reduction. Just sitting back, taking some deep breaths, and thinking about the peace of mind this philosophy brings, fills me with peace and a feeling of total wellness at this moment.

Many social scientists believe that social and psychological aspects of religion may bring about the positive attitudes that increase longevity. However, the greatest enhancer of longevity is believed to be marriage. Widows, especially during the first year of their bereavement, have more symptoms of physical and mental disease than married women, with four times higher death rates. Statistically, married people live longer than single, divorced or widowed people.

People with close-knit, intimate relationships appear to experience less illness than those who do not confide in anyone. People who have at least one confidant who is there for them when a crisis situation arises are able to deal more successfully with difficulties. In other words, they are more stress-resistant. Thus, having at least one best friend and confidant, a person who accepts us as we are, preferably our soulmate, could be the strongest life-saving force for all of us. This person would be the one to share our burdens and our joys, our lows and our highs, one who does not become impatient if we have the need to tell the same story repeatedly.

It may not always be beneficial to keep rehashing unhappy events, because emotions feed on themselves. But sometimes it is necessary to rehash things a bit. This can help to clarify the matter in our own mind. We need to acknowledge our feelings and stresses in order to effectively deal with them. The confidant - and if we are lucky he or she is a good listener - is our partner in this endeavor.

Among living creatures, pets are known to be wonderful antidotes to stress. I can attest to that, because I own a team of Siberian Husky sled dogs. I spend endless hours caring for these furry *best friends*, loving them, training intensely through fall and winter. And this bond increases steadily during sled races, wilderness travel and winter camping trips. *If I'm sad, the devotion in the eyes of these magnificent creatures makes every*thing alright again.

All you really need is one pet you can stroke, while taking deep breaths. This has been shown to reduce the heart rate and blood pressure. I can't think of a more enjoyable quick fix for stress.

Of course, not everyone can have a pet, nor should you go and get one for stress reduction only. If you don't love animals, having a pet will most likely do nothing for you. In fact, the work involved in taking care of the animal will cause you more stress.

For those who do not have a pet, Teddy Bears or other stuffed animals make great substitutes. Hugging such a smiley *critter* tightly can make you feel really good. About twelve years ago my daughter, Cheryl, gave me a stuffed Husky named Laska, and he travels with me wherever I go. Laska has been in Europe more than a dozen times, and lots of other places. I can't imagine traveling without my little Laska, especially when traveling alone.

Handling Anger

Anger is another very real, fundamental human emotion, and in a partnership as close knit as that of a marriage, there seems to be no way to avoid it entirely, no matter how hard we try. Anger is a *legitimate* emotion, designed to gear us up for self-defense if necessary. But if it is released against our soulmates, it is always harmful.

My acquaintance, Tammy, complains that her husband is always nice to others, but at home he "unloads" on her frequently. He lets frustration about things occurring at the office build in him all day long. He never shows anger at his superiors and colleagues. Then, when he comes home, he "explodes" for no apparent reason, making life unpleasant for her and the children.

Tammy usually withdraws and lets her anger at her husband build and build. She has never told him how she feels about his outbursts. And that means she is "training" him to keep "unloading" on her.

This couple urgently needs counseling in the art of communication. He needs to learn to relate his feelings and explain that his outbursts of anger are not meant for her. She needs to learn to tell him, at a time when he is calm, that his outbursts are hurting her. Then, together, they need to work on strategies for future problems, so that they are ready when problems arise.

Diffusing anger is somewhat of a con-troversial subject. Some experts believe in letting it all out, others say expressing anger too vehemently can lead to more stress and sometimes a heart attack.

Understanding why you are angry can help to resolve the anger at its deepest level. This may require some soul searching to determine why you are feeling angry about a certain act, and why the act was committed in the first place. This makes it easier to come to terms with your feelings.

If expressing anger makes you angrier, this could be dangerous. Because, the anger could escalate, establishing a continuously angry attitude, a habit of constant hostility. If you feel yourself getting angrier and angrier after expressing anger, another approach to your anger may be better. For example, keep quiet about momentary irritations. Distract yourself with pleasant thoughts or activities until your fury simmers down.

If you try to distract yourself, chances are that you will feel better faster than if you would have given in to the urge to scream at someone.

Of course it does feel good momentarily to vent your anger at a perceived injustice. For instance, your husband comes home late again, and the nice dinner you have so lovingly prepared is ruined. Naturally you want to tell him how upset you are. But if you do this in your first moments of anger, the words may come out too harsh. You may work yourself up into a *boiling* state of mind. The stress and tension may send your blood pressure *through the roof*, and your heart rate may rise into the danger zone.

Here is where stress perception comes in. Is a ruined dinner worth putting just one more nail into your coffin?

Other experts warn against storing up too much anger. A distinction is believed to exist between *suppressed* and *repressed* anger. Consciously holding back your anger because you don't want to start a fight is suppressed anger. Unconsciously harboring angry feelings toward someone for a long time, perhaps years, is repressed anger.

An example of repressed anger would be

harboring anger against your parents, but never wanting to admit this. Although you may not realize it, this feeling will continue to *fester in your unconscious mind*. *And this* is believed to have the potential to cause greater damage to your health than suppressing anger. In other words, if one consciously holds back anger momentarily, this is less detrimental than unconsciously harboring angry feelings toward someone for a long time.

The professional literature is replete with reports citing studies pointing to the benefits of expressing anger, as well as those describing adverse effects of expressing anger.

So you are faced with forming your own opinion about *blowing your top*. Does it escalate anger and increase stress? Or does it resolve the angry feeling and reduce stress? I believe much of that depends on the individual, the degree of anger, and whether the situation causing it can be resolved.

Perhaps briefly stating your anger, getting it off your chest, and then redirecting your attention elsewhere may be a good way to stay healthy. But if you allow your anger to generate more anger, this prolonged stress could eventually cause serious health problems.

For couples, getting in touch with their true feelings and discussing them openly, without delay, could lead to a satisfactory resolution of a conflict before there is a need to *explode*.

It has been suggested that writing down how you feel about a person or situation that is causing you anger in a diary or just on a piece of paper immediately, will diffuse the anger, and you may forget about it. Recording your feelings and the events that have caused these feelings, can also help you to identify your anger and its source. This, in turn, may bring you closer to a solution of the problem.

We all walk a tightrope when it comes to ways to diffuse anger. We all get angry. There's no way around it. But we owe it to ourselves to try and find a way to regain our inner peace as soon as possible. So don't store it too long.

If you are one of those emotionally hardy people who can just say, "Oh, well, he or she (the person who made you mad) is just being a *jerk*, consider the source" ... then your anger will be brief. Peace returns to your soul quickly, because you just won't let anyone *get to you*. You simply don't allow anyone to hurt you.

But if you are not that hardy and resistant to irritants, and you can *feel* an excessive amount of tension in your body, you may need to have a discussion with the party causing you the anger and try to reach a solution, so that you can relax your nerves.

If the irritant is continual, and you can not resolve your anger by yourself, or you frequently feel angry without a reason, you need to go for help. Immediately, you can talk to a friend, call a crisis hotline or prayer hotline, and then follow this up by finding a counselor. Your doctor's office may be helpful in finding a good counselor.

Support groups are excellent sources for diffusing anger in a peaceful setting where you are not alone. There, you can benefit from the support of the other group members.

If you meet others in the group who have greater problems than yours, this may help you to count your blessings a bit. Support groups are not a total solution, but they can be a good adjunct to other ways of dealing with anger.

More Outlets for Stresses

It is well known that people who have no stress release outlets are more prone to disease. Those who can cope are generally healthier and more resistant to disease.

Tears provide an excellent outlet for stress. For my friend Ann, crying provided release from the shock she felt when her husband left her. After the cry she thought would last forever, she got up feeling much stronger than she had felt in a long time.

It is thought that emotional distress can produce toxic substances within the body, and that crying can help to remove some of these toxins. So there's one more benefit of letting the tears roll. I can't speak for men, but I don't know of any woman who hasn't felt better after a good cry. Do you? There is a reason why we cry, so use the resource if you feel like it.

Most men never cry, and that is unfortunate. As previously discussed, a man is brought up not to show emotion, not to cry, but rather, to show himself strong and in control, even if he is not. Men pay a big price for this, and it is good that modern men are beginning to disregard those antiquated notions and expectations. It is a sign of progress that at least some men have learned to release pent-up emotions by crying. Better to cry than to drink or get in other kinds of trouble.

As already mentioned, stay away from negative thinking. Don't let wrong imaginations take hold of your mind. Of course that's easier said than done. Changing negative thoughts to positive thoughts requires the same amount of discipline as that required of a competitive athlete to condition his or her body.

Maintaining a positive attitude is a continuous process. If the *maintenance work* is not kept up, the mind will *rust*. The destructive thoughts will once again dominate you and make your life miserable.

This is particularly applicable to marriage. When things have gone wrong, the trap of negative thinking is there to catch you and clamp onto you, just like that "instrument of the devil", the leghold trap, wounds and immobilizes animals. Sometimes it takes all of our energy to fight negative thoughts, especially about our partners. You may, at times, have to literally scream at these thoughts, "No, stop it, I am not going to listen to you."

Imagination Can Run Wild

Positive affirmations, instead of negative ones, can go a long way toward stress reduction. You could say to yourself, *My mate loves me and would never be unfaithful,* instead of thinking, *Wonder who he or she is with,* or, *Wonder why that meeting is taking so long?*

An imagination that is too vivid can lead to unfounded jealousy, and unfounded jealousy can destroy a marriage. I said, un*founded* jealousy. If there is a reason to be jealous, that's a different story. Here I'm talking about imagining things that are not true. The mind can go wild once a negative thought takes hold. These thoughts are totally unproductive and they waste energy. They can get you into depression and eventually ruin your health.

So don't let your imagination run away with you. Distract yourself. Harness your creativity by writing a poem or short story, or a letter to a friend you haven't seen in a long time, or whatever else you can think of that's creative. Do not let your creativity go into the direction of negative thinking.

Letting go of imaginations and fears is a difficult process. Your attitude will do a lot for or against you. You need to take control of your life, your stressors, your health. If you have been dwelling on the negative, complaining chronically, always seeing the worst in situations and people, you can change that. It's never too late to start anew.

Attitude

Your attitude toward your surroundings determines how happy your life is. In his book, *The Conquest of Happiness,* Bertrand Russell tells us that the best road to happiness is to spread our interests as wide as possible and have as friendly an attitude as possible toward the people and things around us.

Happiness is a choice, and so is misery. Many factors affect our attitudes and vulnerability to illness, and these include our heredity and our environment. But many researchers are now convinced that the most decisive factors in regard to health or illness are firmly under our control.

In this day and age, where everything that goes wrong is considered *someone else's fault*, it is difficult for people to stop blaming everyone or everything else for all their misfortunes and sicknesses. Many have trouble accepting that some, or rather, most of these, are their own doing.

I believe that health and happiness are God's will for us. What we need to do is accept the notion that we have control, and that the decision to be emotionally hence physically healthy is within our own power.

Make Good Choices in Your Relationships

It is important that people do not set themselves up for misery from the start by choosing the wrong partner for life. In other words, make good choices. I believe that there is a *right* partner for everyone.

When you have found Mr or Ms *Right*, then establish a good and loving communications and mutual support system. With that, plus commitment, honesty, fidelity, and the right <u>attitude</u>, the emotional and physical health of both partners will bloom.

Don't Give Up

If things are not right in your life even after following much of the advice in this book, then ask a professional to help you make the positive changes you want. Don't give up. If you give up, your immune system may just do the same, leaving you a perfect candidate for depression and all the other illnesses caused by stress.

Forgive and Let Go

I have described many, though not all, of the known stress coping or stress reducing methods. One of the most effective, or perhaps the most effective method of stress reduction is forgiving someone who hurt you. This applies especially to the hurt married partners often inflict on each other.

Forgiveness means we release the persons or conditions that bind us to unhappiness. It is also - at least in my mind - the hardest thing one may ever have to do. But it is the one point without which all the other methods won't work very well. You will never be completely restored without this step - the most difficult one - in the healing process. Forgiveness is the subject of the next chapter.

CHAPTER IX

FORGIVENESS

"Lord, make me an instrument of Your peace
where there is hatred, let me sow love
where there is injury, pardon,
where there is doubt, faith
where there is despair, hope
where there is darkness, light
where there is sadness, joy ..."

(By St. Francis of Assisi)

Have you ever said, "I'm sorry," and really meant it? Did you then feel a surge of relief flowing through your body? You are not alone. That is how it feels to humble yourself and ask for forgiveness.

Have you ever said, "I forgive you," and truly meant it? And was this followed by an even greater wave of relief? In fact, did a deep sense of peace come over you after you said these words? Again, you are not the only one who feels that way after forgiving or asking for forgiveness.

On another occasion you may have said, "Why should I forgive?" How did you feel then? Did you feel tense and upset? That's a normal process too. As you have read in the last chapter, too much tension and emotional burdens carried around for too long will eventually affect your health.

Forgiveness is not just for the wrong-doer. Quite often, forgiveness is only for the forgiver, because, in many instances the person you are angry at or hurt by doesn't even know how you feel. Quite often this person doesn't even care whether you forgive

or not. So why carry the burden of unforgiveness around any longer? Why give the
person who hurt you power over you, the
power to continue hurting you because you
can't let go?

In the little book, *The Freeing Power
of Forgiveness*, Unity, School of Christianity, Martha Smock states:

> "Others need your love and blessing, but you,
> more than anyone else, benefit from giving
> expression to forgiving love. This is the way
> of freedom and release. The binding thoughts
> are loosed; the tense muscles are relaxed; the
> taut emotions are quieted. Forgiving, you are
> forgiven. Blessing, you are blessed."

Yes, **forgiveness is for you.** When un-
forgiving thoughts from the past keep you
from experiencing all the joys of life in
the present, you have only one choice: TO
FORGIVE.

Let Go

Forgiveness means letting go of self-
destructive thoughts and emotions, letting
go of what's been dragging you down. Whether
you forgive or not does not change the past,
but it will either *make or break* your
future.

We all know that the most intense of
all pain is that inflicted on us by those we
love, and it is the hardest to forgive. But
try we must, if we want to live and not just
vegetate, wallowing in hurt and resentment
and hate and self-pity.

You may say, "It's impossible, I can't
do it," or, "I've tried, it doesn't work."
Or you may say, "Just how do you propose
that I forgive the one who has destroyed my
life?" These are very normal and legitimate

objections to forgiveness. But try anyway, for your own sake, for your health.

Deeds are done, they can never be undone. Words are spoken, they can never be taken back. How we let these things affect our present and our future, that's up to us.

In her book, *You Can Heal Your Life,* Louise Hay tells us that the past is over, and we cannot change what has happened. But we can change our thoughts about the past. "How foolish," she writes, "for us to punish ourselves in the present moment because someone hurt us in the long ago past."

This author, who experienced the pain of abuse as a child, goes on to say that, in order to release the past, we have to be willing to forgive everyone, including ourselves. Our willingness to forgive starts the healing process.

In Hay's opinion all disease comes from a state of unforgiveness. I agree to an extent, and this is backed up by medical experts saying that up to 90 percent of all illness starts in the head.

Louise Hay suggests that, when we are ill, we should ask ourselves if there is someone we need to forgive. Forgiveness does not mean that you have to condone the behavior that brought you pain. It only means *letting go,* resisting the temptation to hash it over in your mind *endlessly.*

Loving the Self

Louise Hay states that in her counseling practice, when people tell her about their problems, for instance, poor health, unfulfilling relationships, lack of money, there is only one thing she works on. It is **loving the self.** This author claims that when we really love and accept and APPROVE

OF OURSELVES EXACTLY AS WE ARE, then everything in life works.

How easy that sounds. Although it is true that our relationships, our jobs, in fact our whole life works better when we accept and love ourselves first, this is not always so easy. Our self-concept, as discussed in Chapter I, goes back to our childhood. It is an accumulation of memories. It is what we believe of ourselves, how we see ourselves. Since these beliefs about ourselves have been deeply ingrained since early childhood, they are not easily undone. If we do not see ourselves as a person we would approve of, then how can we approve of ourselves?

If our parents have told us we must be perfect in every way, we must not show pain or any other emotions, we must do this and that and that ... and must not do this and that and that, this seems to be very deeply imprinted in our minds. So we feel trapped in the personality our parents and other role models created for us.

This does not mean we should blame our parents, because they only did what their parents did to them. Everything is passed down many generations. Everyone did the best they could under their own circumstances.

So how do you love yourself if you are convinced that you are unlovable, or even objectionable? How do you love someone who let his parents down because he didn't turn out perfect? It's like this. You are not supposed to be perfect. All you are ever asked to do is your best. Whatever that is. And if you haven't always done your best, it only means you are human, like the rest of us.

Those of us who believe in God know that He loves us and forgives us our trespasses, so why shouldn't we love - and forgive - ourselves?

Stop the Criticism

In my zeal to talk about the self-concept and loving the self, it seems as though I'm getting away from the issue of forgiveness. But not really. Because, in order to forgive others, we must first forgive ourselves for whatever we did or said. We must learn to like our imperfect selves, and then we can go on to the next step, to accept others as they are. Only then can the process of forgiving begin, **the process of setting ourselves free, the process of healing our life.**

Loving ourselves and others should begin with the decision to stop criticizing ourselves and others. Because, as I have mentioned before, we can not change others unless they are willing to change. We can change ourselves though. And since criticizing ourselves relentlessly all our lives hasn't worked, it's time to try something else. Approving of ourselves the way we are. This doesn't mean that we should suddenly approve of every rotten thing we ever did. It only means we should forgive ourselves, go on to improve, then forgive others, and give them a chance to change.

If we change our critical ways and forgive, we have a chance to influence others to do the same. If we are not willing to forgive, we might try to just let go of a deed or situation, whatever it may be. **Stop thinking about it!**

Words From a Great Teacher of Love

In his book *Loving Each Other: The Challenge of Human Relationships*, Leo F. Buscaglia states:

> "Forgive. There is a wonderful aura surrounding the verb forgive, great warmth and strength. It is a word suggesting a letting go, a releasing, an action which has the power to soothe, heal, reunite and recreate."

This author, psychologist and educator, goes on to say that forgiving others is a complicated process that "involves our deepest empathy, humanity and wisdom. Historically we have found that without forgiveness there can be no lasting love, no change, no growth, no real freedom."

According to Buscaglia, "forgiveness is an act of will."

The Bible Tells Us to Forgive

The apostle Paul tells us to

> "Get rid of all bitterness, rage and anger," and to "be kind and compassionate to one another, forgiving each other, just as in Christ God forgave you."

(Ephesians 4:31).

Are We Qualified to Judge Others?

We're all guilty of saying and doing little things that hurt and upset others, especially our soulmates. We should be willing to forgive others for the same things, so others may forgive us.

When we want to judge someone else's actions or words, shouldn't we ask ourselves first if we are blameless. Jesus said: "Why do you look at the speck of sawdust in your brother's eye and pay no attention to the plank in your own eye?" (Luke 6:41). So, shouldn't we ask ourselves if we are really qualified to judge the other person? If we would ask ourselves that question, we might find out that we are so stuck on our own biases, that we couldn't possibly be qualified to pass judgment on another person.

So, why not just consider forgiving as a routine process? If we would practice more forgiveness in the small things, forgiveness of bigger things would be easier. I didn't say *easy,* I said **easier.**

Two Friends Struggling to Forgive

I have two friends who are struggling with forgiving. Both are trying. Sometimes they succeed, and at other times they have "relapses". But they keep trying.

The first one, Corinne, is a French lady who now resides in Frankfurt, Germany. We met a long time ago at college and have remained good friends. Corinne has worked for years at forgiving her husband who committed an indiscretion with one of her friends. Corinne loves her husband. Divorce was never an option. But she suffered for a long time after the affair ended. And her health declined steadily during those years.

One day while still in turmoil, she felt a sudden surge of strength, and the motivation and resolve to put her life back together. Corinne claims that she received supernatural strength to pull herself together, to start taking care of herself and restore her failing health, and to begin the forgiving hence healing process. It happened after immersing herself in the Bible and intense prayer for some time. She began to work hard at forgiving and putting her life and her marriage back together. She and her husband worked out their problems and have had a good life ever since.

But the forgiving process is not completed. As of today, Corinne says: "I forgive him, but I still can not forgive her completely. Sometimes I think I have forgiven her, and other times I know I have not." Corinne is a strong, intelligent woman. I know that someday she'll forgive her friend. It may not be until her own or her friend's deathbed. For Corinne's sake, I hope it will be sooner.

The second friend, Nancy, has forgiven her husband, Danny, for having had an affair a few years ago. But "relapses" continue. The "scar tissue over the wound," as she calls it, "keeps acting up." At such times, resentment gets hold of her, and she just wants to do something to hurt Danny. Nancy tries hard to be a loving wife and get along with her husband, and so she does not bring up the past as she had promised him. But sometimes she does something she is not proud of. For example, to counteract her troubled feelings and frustration, she may put extra butter in his food when he should eat a low-fat diet for health reasons. She feels guilty afterward, adding to her own emotional burden.

So it is clear how we are all affected differently. But these two ladies are working hard, and hoping to someday completely forgive. It takes time. And it is very important to work on the willingness to forgive. I believe that if you are willing, God will help you find a way, even if you live through years of bitterness first.

FORGIVENESS

Three Beautiful Children Lose their Mother

An almost forgotten memory comes to mind, that of a man who did not do so well with forgiveness. Years ago a young woman named Karin answered a newspaper ad of mine for a live-in babysitter/housekeeper. Although this young woman appeared troubled, I refrained from asking her why, although later I wished I had. Here is her story.

One day when Michael, Karin's husband came home from working the night shift at his job, he found Karin gone without an explanation, having left their three young children with a babysitter. That was the day Karin answered my ad. Several days after she moved in she told me that she had left a nice man and three beautiful young children, out of pure boredom. How sad, how tragic.

I tried to talk Karin into returning to her husband Michael and the children, but to no avail. She wanted to enjoy her freedom, and she started dating several men. To make a long, dramatic story short, Michael found her. Negotiations to return did not work out because of Karin's stubbornness to hold on to her freedom.

Michael later told me he could forgive her running away, but not "running around with all those guys." When he filed for divorce after several months of *high drama* involving him, Karin and the children, Karin suddenly *woke up* and wanted to return home. Too late. Michael said no. He told me he "will never forgive her." For his sake, I hope he changed his mind.

Forgive and Forget

Forgive and Forget. How often were we told this by our mothers during our childhood when we were angry at friends. It goes

KEEP THE FLAME ALIVE

without saying that, if one could really forget, forgiving should come along automatically. But how? The mind keeps churning away.

People will say, "I can forgive, but I can't forget." Sure, forgetting would make forgiving easier, but maybe complete amnesia would not be such a good idea, either. We may not want to forget a bad experience completely, because we want to be alert not to let it happen again. At the same time we need to control the troubling thoughts when they surface. Perhaps we could acknowledge them briefly, then let them go. **If we dwell on unhappy events of the past, they'll hurt us all over again.**

Distance Yourself from the Experience

Perhaps you could try to distance yourself from the cues that revive the troubling memories in your mind.

An acquaintance of mine, Kathy, solved her problem by physically distancing herself from the source of her troubles. After going through a painful divorce, Kathy's frustration continued because of constant bickering between her and her husband about the support money on which he was often *in arrears*.

Kathy is an intelligent woman and knows that our thoughts and feelings about someone strengthen the invisible bonds - our soul ties - with that person. She knew that she must loose herself from the unhealthy bond. But despite her efforts to forgive, she could not release the constant thoughts about her husband and their problems. *If only I could forget some of the bad things ... maybe I could then forgive and heal my life.*

FORGIVENESS

The solution came during meditation.
Kathy believes God told her to distance herself physically, and the mental part would
follow. She moved away with the children and
hired a contact person to deal with her ex-
husband. Although this was not a quick-fix
solution to all of the problems, it helped
because there were whole days and weeks
during which she never gave him a thought.
Whenever her thoughts wandered back into the
past, she practiced strict self-discipline,
and kept herself from *touching* the situation.

By visualizing that the bad thought was
a dangerous electrical wire, she mustered
the self-discipline to make it disappear.
The healing started, simply because Kathy
worked hard at forgetting many of the unhappy details of the past, making the work
of forgiving a little easier. Slowly but
surely, things got better, both for her and
the children.

So perhaps distancing yourself from a
situation physically, and not letting the
old hurtful thoughts intrude, may be the
first step in the forgiveness process.

Not Every Approach Works for Everyone

Not everything works for everyone. For
me, forgiving becomes easier when I stop
thinking about a wrong, or, what I perceive
as a wrong done me. But not thinking about
it is almost impossible to do, unless the
bad thought is replaced by visualizing better things. Replacing the bad thoughts with
positive, good thoughts works best for me.

First I deal briefly with the situation
if it popps back into my mind, in other
words, I acknowledge it, then I try to let
it go. If it doesn't go away, I tell it
firmly - and I actually speak the words -

"stop, get out." It works for me. This is not to say that *the demons* won't return. But for the moment I have succeeded, and can go on to more productive thinking. If I have to go to my memory bank or my joy list (previously described) and pull out something funny from the past to laugh about, I do it. Putting myself into the *laughing mode* makes forgiving easier.

If I have some forgiving to do, it helps to say the words, "I forgive you for..." Or, "I forgive you because you are just a foolish human being, a product of our time..." Or I may say, "I forgive you because I don't want to carry this grudge around with me any longer." I might even say, "Who are you, Karen, to fault another person, when you are not exactly a saint yourself?"

Charles Fillmore, the founder of Unity, School of Christianity, is said to have taken the time every night to mentally forgive everyone.

Father, Forgive Them

As Jesus hung on the cross, he said, "Father, forgive them." If Christ forgave those who tortured him and then nailed him to the cross, how small it is of us not to forgive. You may say, "I could forgive everything else, but infidelity... no way!" Time heals even those wounds, and by actively trying to forgive, this healing will progress faster.

It is not easy to be disappointed by the person you believed in, whose moral character you thought was impeccable. But it also isn't easy to carry the load of disappointment and resentment in your heart every day. This emotional burden interferes with the progress of your life and may eventually destroy your health.

Do you remember the story from the Bible, where Peter came to Jesus and asked, "Lord, how many times should I forgive my brother if he sins against me? As many as seven times?" (Mt. 18:21). Jesus replied, "Not seven times, but, I tell you, seventy-seven times." (Mt. 18:22).

To me this means that Jesus knew how difficult it was, and that the process of forgiving must be repeated indefinitely, until it works, until you feel its freeing power. If practiced frequently, forgiveness will become more spontaneous in the future.

As we forgive, we should not forget to cultivate our ability to accept forgiveness from others. This means that we need to eliminate the barriers of guilt that stand between us and experiencing the freeing feeling of being forgiven, and accepting ourselves and our imperfections.

Leonardo da Vinci Had Trouble, Too

A story about Leonardo da Vinci says that, in the painting of The Last Supper in the Sistine Chapel in Rome, the famous artist decided to paint the face of a person against whom he carried a long-term grudge onto the face of Judas. He replaced Judas' face with that of his enemy. After he did this, he felt deeply depressed about the ugliness of this deed, and when he tried to paint the face of Jesus, he could not do it. Jesus' face just did not come out right.

So in that instance, this great man's vindictiveness ruined not only his peace of mind, but his skill as an artist as well. After he went to his enemy and forgave him,

KEEP THE FLAME ALIVE

he painted out the insult. Then, he was able
to paint the face of Jesus, and this face is
considered one of the most beautiful in the
world of art.

The moral of this story, of course, is
that unforgiveness gives us misery, and can
rob us of our skills in whatever we do. Do
you want to pay that price? I don't.

"Neither do I Condemn You ..."

The Bible (John 8:11) tells the story
of a woman who had sinned and was brought to
Jesus by the Pharisees. When they quoted the
law of Moses, which states that such women
should be stoned, Jesus said, "If anyone of
you is without sin, let him be the first to
throw a stone at her." After these words all
but the woman left. Jesus then asked the
woman, "Has no one condemned you?" When she
replied, "No," Jesus said, "Neither do I
condemn you."

If you repeat those words often, turning them toward anyone who has hurt you, and
toward any feeling of doubt or uncertainty,
you'll soon begin to feel the release within
you. These words could mean the healing of
your relationships, your health, your life,
if you use them often.

Just as bad words feed on themselves to
produce more negative feelings, these five
wonderful words, "Neither do I condemn
you...," will feed on themselves and become
a routine in your life. They will melt away
nagging pains and promote feelings of peace
and wellness. You will find that everything
in your life will work better, you may even
sleep better. Accept this release now, keep
saying the words, and don't forget to use
them on yourself too.

FORGIVENESS

Easier Said Than Done?

All of this sounds easier said than done. But life wasn't supposed to be easy. As I have already mentioned, forgiving is one of the hardest things to do, and for those who choose the words from the Bible, these words must be spoken over and over.

Jesus knew it wasn't going to happen by forgiving seven times, that's why he said seventy-seven. And you may have to increase that to seven hundred seventy-seven. But keep working. What have you got to lose? Only the burden of hatred and resentment and unforgiveness. And this hurts only you, not the one who did you wrong.

A little booklet called "Daily Word" (page pertaining to June 29, 1995), published by Unity School of Christianity, suggests to make forgiving a daily practice. It states, in part:

> "Rather than trying to forgive every-
> thing at once, we forgive little things
> here and there. Gradually, step-by-step,
> we will find that forgiveness comes
> easier."

Forgiveness is a choice. I hope you make that choice. I hope that your life will be filled with love and forgiveness, and that you will one day forget all the bad times and remember only the good. I hope that healing will take place where needed, and that your marriage will flourish.

CHAPTER X

KEEP THE FIRE BURNING

This is the Chapter you've been waiting for! It is a sum-up of what has already been said in previous chapters, plus more. This chapter is meant to be a prescription for keeping love, hence joy, alive, 'til death do us part'.

All human beings need to feel loved and accepted, **every day.** Valentine's Day, birthdays, anniversaries and special occasions are not enough. Love needs to be expressed often, both in words and in deeds.

Defining Love

Love has been defined thousands of times. I don't think anyone could possibly come up with a new definition. One that appealed to me, especially, appeared in the booklet, *Living by the Spirit*, by J. Sig Paulson, Unity, School of Christianity. It goes like this:

> "Love is to appreciate, to revere, to worship, to be grateful, to respect, to serve. The true nature of love will unfold as you keep this commandment."

The Bible defines love as follows (1 Corinthians 13:4-8):

"Love is patient, love is kind. It does not envy, it does not boast, it is not proud. It is not rude, it is not self-seeking, it is not easily angered, it keeps no record of wrongs. Love does not delight in evil but rejoices with the truth. It always protects, always trusts, always hopes, always perseveres. Love never fails....."

Romance

Romance is often defined as only the *icing on the cake* of relationships. To me this means that romance is not all we need for a good marriage. In fact, romance will wear off over the years, while love deepens, or at least should deepen. With the passage of time - after getting to know each other's faults and idiosyncrasies - we enter into a new stage of love and romance, a deepening of our love.

This is not to say that we should not try to keep romance alive if we want icing on our cake. And who doesn't? So we must work at it. We must also realize that our efforts will not always be successful, and that there will be troubled times during which romance is not very much alive.

Most couples are *madly in love* when they marry. Romance runs high at that time. But after a few years have gone by, couples often find themselves wondering where romance went. People get caught up in the stresses of daily living, and often make everything and everyone else their highest priority, when their mate should be Number One. We take each other for granted, and one day we wake up to an empty feeling. "What happened to our romance?"

It's not too late to stir up the embers, perhaps to a cheery gentle fire, perhaps to a roaring flame. That depends on the attitude of the partners. How hard each is willing to work, how many positive things they will do for each other.

Keep in mind that romance is not everything in a marriage, and it does not "fix" more deep-seated problems. It can nevertheless brighten the whole picture, break the monotony, increase intimacy and security, and affirm that the union is forever.

To those who say, "But I am not the romantic type," I say, "Just imagine you are! Try it. You'll find it works." Try to be more lighthearted, to play more, laugh more, dance more often, dine by candle light and romantic music more often. Plan some getaway weekends, just the two of you. All these things can add up to making you feel more romantic, hence increasing romance in your marriage.

The words "dance more often", above, bring to mind a couple who did just that. In fact, their decision to take up ballroom dancing changed their unromantic, uneventful 25-year marriage into a romantic, exciting one.

Rhonda and Allan's son and daughter were away at college. The couple had an "average" marriage. Occasional dinners out or a movie, church most Sundays, watching the fourth of July parade and fireworks. For the most part their lives centered around their jobs and television. They had grown apart and were bored with life and each other. Their sex life was *in a rut* as well.

Then a ballroom dance group formed in their small town. Rhonda, long dissatisfied with her unromantic marriage and boring life, became excited. After much persuasion Allan agreed to join the dance group. The couple had not danced in decades but quickly refreshed what they once did well, and added many new steps.

Soon this couple became members of a demonstration group that occasionally performs at community functions. They are even thinking of entering competition someday. Rhonda enjoys wearing beautiful special dresses on these occasions, and Allan can't take his eyes off her.

It had been many years since Allan called Rhonda his *princess*. According to Rhonda, "It felt so good to hear those words again." Her husband's compliments made her feel young and beautiful. (A wise person once said, "A woman is as beautiful as she feels"). The festive evenings, the rhythm and the physical closeness of dancing became a wonderful new focus in this couple's life. Once again, Allan and Rhonda had something to talk about, to practice and prepare for and look forward to. Something that increased their bonding as a couple.

So, maybe romance is not everything, but for these two people, rekindling romance through dancing certainly added a big plus to their marriage. An added bonus: Increased physical fitness and agility.

Of course, there are many other activities to consider if dancing is not for you. For instance, regular long walks, skiing, camping. The possibilities are endless. All of them have one common denominator. They increase bonding, and they can add to the rekindling of romance if pursued regularly and with enthusiasm.

Most people have heard the phrase: *The family that prays together stays together.* To that I would like to add the phrase: *The family that **plays** together stays together.* At least it has a better chance. So, remain playmates, the way you used to be when you first fell in love, and watch romance come alive.

The Love Bank Account

As mentioned in Chapter VII, in his analogy of the "love bank account" described in the book, *His Needs, Her Needs: How Affair-proof Is Your Marriage?* author Willard F. Harley, Jr., explains that deposits and withdrawals are constantly made. This means that, if you do something positive for your partner, it is a deposit in the account your partner keeps in your name. If you do something that displeases your partner, it is a withdrawal. You may have forgotten about the negative deposits you have made into this account in the past, but the "bank" doesn't forget. In the same way, you keep an account in your partner's name.

If insufficient deposits are made, and the account goes down to zero, you are not in good standing. If you overdraw - in other words, keep making withdrawals when the account is already on zero or below - you are in trouble with your mate, and you may not even realize it. Thus it goes without saying that working on awareness of your actions and words, and even watching your body language toward your partner, can not be overemphasized.

In order to build and maintain a strong relationship it is necessary for both partners to make as many deposits into the "bank account" as possible. Treat your partner well and do as many nice things for him or her as possible. This includes always communicating, always relating, verbalizing your love and need for each other often, especially at times of failure and discouragement. It also means being honest, and sharing fears, failures, dreams and hopes with each other.

Last but not least, the partners must keep their original commitment to each other, and be determined to stick together when adversities come, rather than give up on each other and the marriage.

Bridges

An excellent analogy was described in Dr. James Dobson's *Focus on the Family* Bulletin of June 1995. This analogy compares marriage with bridges. Why bridges? The Bulletin refers to the two thousand year old Roman bridges that are still standing, even though they were constructed with unreinforced stone and mortar. The reason these bridges are still standing is because they are only used for foot traffic. If heavy trucks would pass over them, they would crumble.

So it is with a marriage that is not built on solid values and commitment. This means that after the starry-eyed notions of courtship and honeymoon fade away, maintenance on the "bridge" must continue or it will crumble under pressure, as a Roman bridge would crumble if an 18-wheeler would roll across it. While working on maintenance, couples need to work on protection as well. Protection from what? From **intruders**, of course.

Growing Hedges

This is where the concept of *growing hedges* around your relationship, described in the book titled, *Loving Your Marriage Enough to Protect It,* by Jerry Jenkins, enters into the picture. One of the main points this author makes is avoiding the opportunity for lust to take hold of you. Jenkins makes it clear that spending time alone with a member of the opposite sex, other than one's spouse, should be avoided.

This reminds me of a time when I was traveling for a large company. If men and women had to travel together, the seating arrangements on the plane were always made far apart, and rooms were reserved in different hotels, or at least on different floors. It was an unwritten company rule. No one ever talked about it.

Once we have built the protective hedge around our marriage, we can work on the myriad other things we can do to keep our love for each other alive.

I believe part of the hedge building process includes keeping up a lively interest in, and admiration for each other, so no *outsider* is encouraged to provide these ego strokes. This may include noticing, say, new clothes and new hair cuts or hair styles, or something your partner did well. Because, if partners do not provide this gratification to each other, in other words, maintain the *hedge* properly, *intruders* may enter.

When we talk about intruders we usually mean another person. But your own *wrong thinking* can also be an *intruder* wreaking havoc in your relationship. Some of these intruders come in the form of lust for someone outside of the marriage, as mentioned by Jenkins. Intruders may also come in the form of negative thinking about your partner and your relationship.

Thoughts determine emotions, and emotions, if left alone, can run rampant and cause trouble. So, as mentioned in previous chapters, watch your thoughts closely, and cut off wrong ones.

And ladies, being attractive and fun to be with is a great hedge builder in itself. For example, why would a man allow someone else to intrude if no one could *hold a candle* to his wife? And that goes for both sexes.

Prevention Better Than The Cure

Yes prevention is the best alternative. Divorce prevention works the same as disease prevention. If you heard of some deadly, contagious disease going around, wouldn't you take every precaution, and go to great lengths to protect yourself and your family from contracting it? Divorce is such a disease. And the good news is that you can prevent it from happening to you.

I once asked a young mother with two babies and a part-time job, if she ever worried about her marriage while investing almost all of her time in the children and her job, and almost none in her husband. The reply was, "Right now I worry about raising the kids and balancing the budget. Everything and everyone else can wait." This woman's attitude characterizes many women in similar situations. The sad fact is, if a husband and wife do not make the effort to spend quality time together, drifting apart is inevitable.

Don't let it happen to you. Increase the deposits in that **bank account** and keep growing those **hedges**. And if you haven't planted that hedge and disease has already intruded, don't give up. Chances are, it can be cured.

Make Partner Number One Focus

It has been said that "Marriage is not something you get, it's something you do." **Something you do.** How well said. It means you need to invest a lot of time in your marriage. As already mentioned, you need to pay more attention to each other, do more positive things for each other. Surprise each other with gifts and flowers more often. In other words, keep making those deposits in the *love bank account*.

Do I hear protests? "Who's got the time and the energy?" Consider this. If we worked as hard at improving our marriage partnerships as we do at our jobs and businesses, there would be fewer divorces. And if we were as nice to our spouses as we are to outsiders - especially those of the opposite sex - there would be considerably less marital dissatisfaction, strife and conflict.

But sadly, we often make our marriage partner the last one on the totem pole, when he or she should be FIRST. We need to make more time for our marriages, even if we have to set some other activity or person back. So when our hectic world tries to crowd out messages of love between you and your partner, don't give in, fight it.

We are all different. Not everyone needs the same amount of attention and affection. Speaking for myself, I need a lot of it, and I give it all back. That's the wonderful thing about love. The more you give it away, the more it multiplies.

Needs

In the book, *His Needs, Her Needs: How Affair-proof Is Your Marriage?*, Willard F. Harley, Jr. states that males and females have five basic needs, and these are different for the sexes. Each partner must make the effort to recognize the other's needs. It goes without saying that partners must state their needs clearly, to avoid guesswork and wrong assumptions.

Harley makes it clear that, if any of a spouse's five basic needs are not met, that spouse becomes vulnerable to the temptation of an affair. Based on this author's assessment, then, meeting your partner's needs is one of the most important factors in helping your marriage not only to survive but to thrive.

What are the five basic needs? According to Harley, the five basic needs of the male are sexual fulfillment, recreational companionship, an attractive spouse, domestic support, and admiration. The female's five basic needs are affection, conversation, honesty and openness, financial support, and family commitment.

As a female - although I consider myself physically and emotionally *hardy* and self-sufficient - I do claim most of those five basic needs, and could add a few more. For instance, romance ranks high on my list, and I still like my husband to open doors for me and shield me from traffic when we walk along a street.

Although most of these points have been discussed in other chapters, I feel they are worth repeating. One can not overemphasize that each partner should be aware of the other's needs every day. Do keep in mind that there are individual variations and that some needs may change over time. So be observant, keep up your awareness.

Communicate your own special needs to your partner often, in a nice way, not as demands. If you think of yourself as a poor communicator, improve! This skill can be learned. The success of your marriage depends on it. Use every opportunity to meet your partner's needs. Bring the ones you can not meet up for discussion, in order to find solutions or work on compromises together.

Never leave your partner to his or her own devices when he or she has problems to work out. Offer help so someone else won't have a chance to do so. Believe me, there is always someone of the opposite sex readily available.

Watching out for *helpful* members of the opposite sex is not unreasonable jealousy, only a precaution. Even *best friends* can become too *helpful* to your mate. If partners would communicate properly and share their feelings with each other, there should be no need to discuss them with an outsider and run the danger of becoming involved.

Marital Intimacy

Intimacy means many things, mostly having to do with sharing your most secret feelings, sharing both your joys and your sorrows. And why not share both? Sharing your joys will multiply them, sharing your sorrows will diminish them.

You may say, "What's so special about that?" Hold on. Many couples share neither. A male acquaintance told me, "She doesn't care if my bowling league wins or loses, and I don't care how last Wednesday's bridge game came out, either. We go our separate ways, and we do get along."

I believe that marriage has "died in the mist," and the partners don't even know it. I would also venture to say that both have a deep yearning to share with someone, and sooner or later this will occur. Lack of interest in each other's activities and lack of sharing will eventually drive a couple apart.

Some people are mysterious in nature, always holding something back about themselves. This is fine during courtship, but once you are married, there should be no secrets.

If you are one of those who say, "No mystery, no excitement," there are many things you can do to change that. You can do "mysterious" things to surprise your mate. For instance, gifts, drawing a surprise bubble bath, Valentine's Day or Halloween surprises, maybe a surprise birthday party, if your partner likes that sort of thing. (Some people don't like surprise parties).

These little "mysteries" can spice up a marriage, while you share the serious matters with your mate. Some people may go as far as sharing their successes and their joys with their partners, but not the low points. Why carry a burden without asking for support? Show your mate confidence by sharing *everything*. You should feel accepted enough to share even things you are not proud of.

If you are the non-relating type and you feel you are happy that way, then think of your partner. As already mentioned, body language accounts for a high percentage of human communication. This means that if you are feeling troubled, your body gestures may show this, and your partner may think you are hiding something. Partners, especially females with their *right brain intuitive-*ness, will sense it and may feel hurt by your lack of sharing.

Your mate may even think you are hiding something serious. Better to muster the courage and become vulnerable. And if you do not feel accepted after sharing your feelings with your partner, then your marriage may need some repair. Hopefully you will only need short-term couples counseling to get you both on the right track of sharing and accepting. What's the alternative? You'll drift apart more every day.

We live in the age of mounting garbage. People - and Americans are considered world leaders in this habit - like to throw things away. We always aim for something new. Older things usually are not treated with the care with which we treat newer possessions.

For example, do you treat your 5-year-old car the way you would treat a new car? Inspecting for little scratches and nicks, polishing polishing polishing. Most likely you worry where you park it, put an anti-theft device in it, and insure it well. You probably yell at your kids for leaving toys and crumbs on the seats. Would you give all that special consideration to an older car?

So it is often with our mates, at least in some marriages, fortunately not all.

Happy Couples

I know some happy couples who have been married for 50 years or more. My in-laws Ruth and Elden Gadke fall into this category. Unfortunately, my own mother became a widow when I was only five years old. She never re-married.

Ruth and Elden have been married for 56 years. They hold hands at every opportunity. They treat each other with love and respect. They go everywhere together. They talk with each other endlessly, they share everything, both joy and sorrow, wellness and illness. These two people have never been apart for more than 12 hours at a time in their entire married life. Yet they are not possessive of each other.

I once asked my mother-in-law if that wasn't a little boring .... to be together all the time? She replied with an emphatic, actually, an angry "NO". I never mentioned it again.

Another couple, Ed and Bernice, have been married for more than 60 years. He treats her like a queen, she treats him like a king. When they are away from each other, they brag endlessly about each other's virtues. I asked Bernice as to the "secret" of her wonderful relationship. "Give and take," she said. I wanted to know more, and she again said, "Give and take, that's all."

I know many other loving *old folks*, and hope that's how Richard and I will be someday. And I wish the same for you. But unless we all work hard at it, that is not going to happen. If we don't work at our marriages, it could well be that the aches and pains and frailties of advancing age of a partner will get on the other's nerves. In fact, I do know couples that fall into this category. Quite often they barely tolerate each other.

Case in Point

This brings to mind a story I read a few years ago, which is both sad and funny. It is about an 80-year-old man who was pulled out of a ditch on the Alaska Highway. His car had slid into the ditch and he was hypothermic when he was found. His rescuers warmed him, fed him, then gave him all sorts of advice on how to get safely home to the lower *forty eight*. "Are you kidding?" said the feisty old man, "I went through all this to get away from the *old lady, I'm going NORTH, and* I'm never going back."

Problem Solving

Bernice's statement - "Give and take" - should be the cornerstone of problem solving in a relationship. If you have built strong bridges and maintained a substantial balance in the *love bank account*, problems, when they do arise, will be easier to solve.

If you have a problem, don't try to solve it alone. Let your partner in on it. He or she may feel left out if you don't. On the other hand, much support will come to you if you share. Don't cheat yourself of that help because of pride, or whatever reason you may have to shut your mate out.

If you think your mate is not a good listener, make her or him aware of this in a nice way. Communicate your wish for better listening skills.

If your partner shares a problem with you, be the best listener you can be, and offer advice only if asked. Because, in most cases, a listening ear is all your mate needs. If advice is needed, he or she will ask for it. **Listening attentively is one of the greatest gifts you can give your mate.**

If you follow the guidelines of the previous chapters, there should be fewer marital crises, but some may still occur. Likewise, if you follow these guidelines, you should be better prepared for handling crises.

Conflicts are best worked out when you put yourself in your partner's shoes, try to understand that your partner may feel differently about certain issues. Try to understand that your mate's needs often are not the same as yours. Try to understand the inherent differences between the sexes.

Don't let anger get out of control. Whatever the problem that aroused your anger, try to work things out peaceably. Don't give up on your marriage. You and your mate are still the same people you were years ago. Just that so many things have happened, so many things have come between you.

Perhaps both "relationship accounts" have a zero balance right now, but that can change. Don't throw your marriage away. You have built a history together. Take out your wedding album and other scrapbooks. Look at them together. Talk about "Back when ...." Doesn't that stir some emotions? You could not be totally cold toward each other. Something is still there.

Wake up that something. Cultivate it, and cultivate some humility. Don't be too proud to accept your part of the responsibility for what has happened over the years.

As quoted from the Bible at the beginning of this chapter ... "Love does not insist on its own way ..." Have the courage to be wrong. Have the courage to change. If you change, chances are your partner will too. Not overnight, of course, but over time.

I remember some stormy days in my marriage some years back. Although it did not come up for discussion, the possibility of divorce was heavy on my mind. Because, not having the insight, understanding and tolerance I have today, I too almost became a victim of our throwaway society, of the "me first" ideology.

At that time I simply thought, *Who needs this aggravation ... I'll do OK on my own.* But then, one day, I found myself looking at the beautiful diamond Richard gave me at a time when he could certainly not afford its quality and size. And so many different thoughts and feelings came over me .... I could not even describe them. Some of these feelings centered around the ring. Not its monetary value, but the love connected with it ... all the years ... all we experienced together, the family history we built. And I thought, *Karen, you fool, you were thinking of trashing it all.* Needless to say, I *woke up and smelled the coffee.* I'm glad I did. I made a few changes in myself, and I worked on accepting things I couldn't change in my husband.

Talking yourself into a divorce you might regret can happen very quickly. All you need to do is mention the word, and your partner may take you up on it. Once the ball is rolling, both of you may be too proud to back down. So think it over before you let the word **divorce** out of your mouth.

Acceptance

Accepting the other's little idiosyncrasies and moods means allowing him or her to be human, as we all are. And if you have to criticize, do it in a helpful manner. Yes, if we want to enjoy our relationships, we must accept our partners as they are. We all have flaws. The only unflawed person who ever walked on this earth was Jesus Christ.

I think everyone would agree with the comment made by renowned psychologist Carl Rogers, that one does not watch a beautiful sunset, and then demand that it make slight changes in color here and there. So why do we criticize our partners so relentlessly? We all have fallen into this trap at one time or another. It is easy. We want our lives to be as close to perfect as possible, and it is so much easier to blame others for things gone wrong. Time to accept 50-50 responsibility for anything occurring in our marriages, both good and bad.

So focus on the strengths of your partner, consider your relationship a "work in progress", and accept your partner as he or she is. If you want changes, then lead the way yourself.

See Only the Good in Each Other

A Dostoevsky quote comes to mind here:

"To love someone means to see them as God intended."

God intended for all people to be beautiful. I think everyone agrees with me that it is not the outer shell that really counts, but what's inside. You are beautiful, your partner is beautiful. If we could all believe that, rather than to see only each other's faults, what wonderful marriages we would have.

So, look for the good in your partner instead of criticizing. Build your mate's self esteem instead of tearing it down. Holding back on criticism is even more important if you live with a person with low self esteem. The ego of a person with low self esteem is so fragile, he or she needs more encouragement than the average person. Make your mate feel comfortable, adequate, notice what he or she does right, and ignore the rest, if possible.

To repeat my words from other chapters, be generous with the ego strokes, and never forget to say *thank you* for things your mate does for you.

As I have already mentioned, it is important to control your thoughts and not dwell on the negative. It is hard to see the good and the beauty in the person we share our home with when we know all of his or her faults. And it is so easy to compare our partners with outsiders who show us only their best side. This is one of the reasons it is so easy to fall in love, but harder to stay in love.

Make Your Mate Your Best Friend

The following poem by Nora M. Bozeman was published in New Hope Books, a Salesian Missions publication:

> "A friend is one who's on your side
> Someone in whom you can confide.
> One who consoles you when you're sad
> And turns depressing days to glad.
> A friend is there through thick and thin,
> Caring, concerned and genuine.
> A special someone with the gift
> To give your heart a lift.
> When you're down and in despair
> A faithful friend is always there.
> They do not scold or reprimand
> And always seem to understand.
> So, if you have but one true friend
> To be there for you to the end,
> Thank the Lord and say a prayer -
> You're richer than a millionaire."

If you have one friend who fits every line in the beautiful poem, above, you are indeed lucky. If you have such a friend, it is also very likely that this person is your soulmate. Because, no outsider will ever have your best interests in mind as will your wife or husband. In fact, some friends prefer to be with you only when you are "up". But who is really at your side when you are "down", or ill? Who puts up with your idiosyncrasies, your moods? With rare exceptions, it is your soulmate who sticks with you through thick and thin, in sickness and in health.

That's why the institution of marriage is so wonderful. **"And the two shall become one."**

So be each other's best friend. Feel secure and protected.

Final Words

Now, if you still have doubts whether your marriage can survive and thrive when marriages are under attack from so many evil forces, I believe it can. But you pay a price. The price is called **hard work**. If you want to share in the rewards, just follow the advice in this book and other good books on the subject of relationships, especially when it comes to sharing, honesty, fidelity, and meeting your soulmate's needs.

So, keep loving, keep sharing, keep relating, and *keep the flame alive, 'til death do you part.'*

Thank you for taking the time to read my words. GOD BLESS YOU AND YOUR MARRIAGE!

REFERENCES/RECOMMENDED READING

BOOKS

Bach, George R., and Wyden, Peter. *The Intimate Enemy: How to Fight Fair in Love and Marriage*. New York. Avon Book Co. 1983.

Berne, Eric. *Games People Play*. New York. Grove Press, 1964.

Bloomfield, Harold H., M.D., & Cooper, Robert K., Ph.D. *The Power of 5: Hundreds of 5-Second to 5-Minute Scientific Short-cuts to Ignite Your Energy, Burn Fat, Stop Aging and Revitalize Your Love Life*. Emmaus, Pa: Rodale Press, 1995.

Buscaglia, Leo F., Ph.D. *Living Loving and Learning:* New York. A Fawcett Columbine Book. Published by Ballantine Books, 1985.

Buscaglia, Leo F., Ph.D. *Loving Each Other: The Challenge of Human Relationships*. New York. A Fawcett Columbine Book. Published by Ballantine Books, 1984.

Butterworth, Eric. *In The Flow of Life*. New York, Evanston, San Francisco, London. Harper & Row, 1975.

Capps, Charles. *The Tongue, A Creative Force*. Tulsa, Oklahoma. Harrison House, 1976.

Dyer, Wayne W. *Erroneous Zones*. New York. Funk and Wagnalls. 1991.

Ellis, Albert, Ph.D., and Harper, Robert A., Ph.D. *A New Guide to Rational Emotive Living*. Hollywood, California. Wilshire Book Co. 1975.

Fromme, Allan: *The Ability to Love*. Hollywood, California. Wilshire Book Co., 1965.

References/Recommended Reading, Cont'd

Harley, Willard J., Jr. *His Needs, Her Needs: How Affair-proof Is Your Marriage?* Grand Rapids, Michigan. Fleming H. Revell, a Division of Baker Book House Company. 1986, 1994.

Hay, Louise L. *You Can Heal Your Life.* Santa Monica, California. Hay House, Inc., 1984, 1987.

Holy Bible: New International Version. Colorado Springs, Co. International Bible Society, 1973, 1978, 1984.

Jenkins, Jerry. *Loving Your Marriage Enough to Protect It. Chicago, Illinois. Moody Press-*A Ministry of Moody Bible Institute. 1993.

Jones, James W. *In the Middle of This Road We Call Our Life.* Scranton, Pennsylvania. Harper Collins Publishers. 1995.

Kennedy, Eugene. *A Time For Being Human.* Chicago, Illinois. The Thomas Moore Press. 1977.

LeShan, Lawrence. *How to Meditate: A Guide to Self-Discovery.* Toronto, New York, London, Sydney, Auckland. Bantam Books. 1974.

Living by the Spirit. Part by J. Sig. Paulson. Unity Village, Missouri. Unity School of Christianity. 1995.

McConnell, James V. *Understanding Human Behavior.* 5th ed. New York. Holt, Rinehart and Winston, 1986.

Miller, Lyle H. *The Stress Solution: An* Action Plan to Manage Your Life. New York. Pocket Books. 1993.

New Hope Books. *True Wealth.* Poem titled,"A *True Friend," by* Nora M. Bozeman. New Rochelle, New York. A Salesian Missions Publication. 1996.

References/Recommended Reading, Cont'd

Powell, John. *Why Am I Afraid to Tell You Who I Am: Insights on Self-awareness, Personal Growth and Interpersonal Communication*. Tabor Publishers. 1989.

Rainey, Dennis & Barbara. *Building Your Mate's Self Esteem*. Nashville, Tennessee. Thomas Nelson Publishers. 1986.

Russell, Bertrand. *The Conquest of Happiness*. New York. Liveright Publishing Co. 1930, 1958.

Sheehy, Gail. *Passages: Predictable Crises of Adult Life*. Toronto, New York, London, Sydney, Auckland. Bantam Books. 1976.

The Freeing Power of Forgiveness. Part by Martha Smock. Unity Village, Missouri. Unity School of Christianity. 1995.

MAGAZINES

Daily Word. Unity Village, Missouri.

Dobson, James, Ph.D. Dr. James Dobson's Focus on the Family Bulletin. Mt. Morris, Illinois. Tyndale House Publishers. June 1995.

Marriage Magazine. Saint Paul, Minnesota. International Marriage Encounter, Inc.

New Man. For Men of Integrity. Lake Mary, Florida. Strang Communications Co.

Prevention. Emmaus, Pennsylvania. Rodale Press.

Reader's Digest. Pleasantville, New York. The Reader's Digest Association.

RADIO PROGRAM

Dr. James Dobson's Focus on the Family. Colorado Springs, Colorado. Aired on many stations (1-800-A-FAMILY).

SPECIAL ACKNOWLEDGMENTS

I am pleased to acknowledge permission to reprint brief quotations or describe concepts from the following works:

Buscaglia, Leo F., Ph.D. *Loving Each Other: The Challenge of Human Relationships*. New York. A Fawcett Columbine Book. Published by Ballantine Books, 1984.

Dobson, James, Ph.D. *Dr. James Dobson's Focus on the Family Bulletin*. Mt. Morris, Illinois. Tyndale House Publishers. June 1995.

Harley, Willard J., Jr. *His Needs, Her Needs: How Affair-proof Is Your Marriage?* Grand Rapids, Michigan. Fleming H. Revell, a Division of Baker Book House Company. 1986, 1994.

Holy Bible: New International Version. Colorado Springs, Colorado. International Bible Society, 1973, 1978, 1984.

Jenkins, Jerry. *Loving Your Marriage Enough to Protect It*. Chicago, Illinois. Moody Press-A Ministry of Moody Bible Institute. 1993.

Jones, James W., Ph.D. *In the Middle of This Road We Call Our Life*. Scranton, Pennsylvania. Harper Collins Publishers. 1995.

Living by the Spirit. Part by J. Sig. Paulson. Unity Village, Missouri. Unity School of Christianity. 1995.

New Hope Books. *True Wealth*. Poem titled, "A True Friend," by Nora M. Bozeman. New Rochelle, New York. A Salesian Missions Publication. 1996.

The Freeing Power of Forgiveness. Part by Martha Smock. Unity Village, Mo. Unity School of Christianity. 1995.

Unity School of Christianity, Publisher of *Daily Word*, Unity Village, Mo. June, 1995.